Suicide

Other books in the Current Controversies series

Suicide

Paul Connors, Book Editor

GREENHAVEN PRESS

An imprint of Thomson Gale, a part of The Thomson Corporation

Detroit • New York • San Francisco • New Haven, Conn. • Waterville, Maine • London

THOMSON

---★--- ™

GALE

Christine Nasso, *Publisher*
Elizabeth Des Chenes, *Managing Editor*

© 2007 Thomson Gale, a part of The Thomson Corporation.

Thomson and Star logo are trademarks and Gale and Greenhaven Press are registered trademarks used herein under license.

For more information, contact:
Greenhaven Press
27500 Drake Rd.
Farmington Hills, MI 48331-3535
Or you can visit our Internet site at http://www.gale.com

Cover photograph reproduced by permission of Jennifer Wahi, Art Director.

LIBRARY OF CONGRESS CATALOGING-IN-PUBLICATION DATA

Suicide / Paul Connors, book editor.
  p. cm. -- (Current controversies)
Includes bibliographical references and index.
ISBN-13: 978-0-7377-2488-2 (hardcover) -- ISBN-13: 978-0-7377-2489-9 (paperback)
1. Suicide--Moral and ethical aspects--Juvenile literature. I. Connors, Paul G.
HV6545.S8316 2007
179.7--dc22
                                                        2007001989

ISBN-10: 0-7377-2488-9 (hardcover)
ISBN-10: 0-7377-2489-7 (paperback)

Printed in the United States of America
10 9 8 7 6 5 4 3 2 1

Contents

Chapter 2: What Are the Causes of Suicide?

Chapter 3: Should Physicians Help Terminally Ill Patients Commit Suicide?

Yes: The Terminally Ill Have a Right to Physician-Assisted Suicide

As Americans enter the "Age of Aging," the number of individuals suffering from the indignities of old age continues to soar. There is no solution to the problems of debility and death, and modern medicine cannot miraculously cure aging loved ones.

Chapter 4: How Can Suicide Be Prevented?

Foreword

By definition, controversies are "discussions of questions in which opposing opinions clash" (Webster's Twentieth Century Dictionary Unabridged). Few would deny that controversies are a pervasive part of the human condition and exist on virtually every level of human enterprise. Controversies transpire between individuals and among groups, within nations and between nations. Controversies supply the grist necessary for progress by providing challenges and challengers to the status quo. They also create atmospheres where strife and warfare can flourish. A world without controversies would be a peaceful world; but it also would be, by and large, static and prosaic.

The Series' Purpose

The purpose of the Current Controversies series is to explore many of the social, political, and economic controversies dominating the national and international scenes today. Titles selected for inclusion in the series are highly focused and specific. For example, from the larger category of criminal justice, Current Controversies deals with specific topics such as police brutality, gun control, white collar crime, and others. The debates in Current Controversies also are presented in a useful, timeless fashion. Articles and book excerpts included in each title are selected if they contribute valuable, long-range ideas to the overall debate. And wherever possible, current information is enhanced with historical documents and other relevant materials. Thus, while individual titles are current in focus, every effort is made to ensure that they will not become quickly outdated. Books in the Current Controversies series will remain important resources for librarians, teachers, and students for many years.

In addition to keeping the titles focused and specific, great care is taken in the editorial format of each book in the series. Book introductions and chapter prefaces are offered to provide background material for readers. Chapters are organized around several key questions that are answered with diverse opinions representing all points on the political spectrum. Materials in each chapter include opinions in which authors clearly disagree as well as alternative opinions in which authors may agree on a broader issue but disagree on the possible solutions. In this way, the content of each volume in Current Controversies mirrors the mosaic of opinions encountered in society. Readers will quickly realize that there are many viable answers to these complex issues. By questioning each author's conclusions, students and casual readers can begin to develop the critical thinking skills so important to evaluating opinionated material.

Current Controversies is also ideal for controlled research. Each anthology in the series is composed of primary sources taken from a wide gamut of informational categories including periodicals, newspapers, books, U.S. and foreign government documents, and the publications of private and public organizations. Readers will find factual support for reports, debates, and research papers covering all areas of important issues. In addition, an annotated table of contents, an index, a book and periodical bibliography, and a list of organizations to contact are included in each book to expedite further research.

Perhaps more than ever before in history, people are confronted with diverse and contradictory information. During the Persian Gulf War, for example, the public was not only treated to minute-to-minute coverage of the war, it was also inundated with critiques of the coverage and countless analyses of the factors motivating U.S. involvement. Being able to sort through the plethora of opinions accompanying today's major issues, and to draw one's own conclusions, can be a complicated and frustrating struggle. It is the editors' hope that Current Controversies will help readers with this struggle.

Introduction

Demographics suggest that the current
trend to rationalize and glamorize suicide will continue to move our national
culture in a pro-suicide direction.

Increasingly, Americans are acknowledging that suicide is becoming an almost common—albeit divisive—phenomenon
in our national culture. Intentional self-harm or suicide was
once regarded as a private affair, involving an undoubtedly
immoral and irrational decision. There is an important strain
in Christian and Jewish tradition that cherishes life as a gift
from God, not an individual choice. The euphemism "Culture
of Life" holds that human life, at all stages from conception
through natural death, is sacred. Many who hold these beliefs
also argue that suicidal urges are indications of mental illness
and that therefore self-destruction can hardly be considered a
rational act. Moreover, because suicide is an irreversible act, it
is in the best interest of those considering it that society protect them from themselves. Therefore, opponents of suicide
are opposed to all practices they see as destructive of human
life, including physician-assisted suicide (PAS) and euthanasia.

Today, the nation is growing openly pro-suicide. Intentional self-harm is glamorized by Hollywood and in pop culture. The 2004 Academy Award–winning movie *Million Dollar
Baby* depicted a prizefighter paralyzed from the neck down.
Not wanting to live any longer, she convinced a friend to help
her commit assisted suicide. Critics of the PG-13 film com-
plained that the picture offered a right-to-die message to im-
pressionable youths. The movie was also condemned by disability rights activists, who argued the film preached a "better
dead than disabled" message. Pro-life advocates complain that
pop culture is sympathetic to suicide. Increasing incidents of

cluster suicides among teenagers across the nation are an indication that these victims view self-initiated death as a fad not unlike hairstyles, slang, and pop music. Not only is suicide glamorized, but it is seen as both a moral and rational decision. The PAS and euthanasia movements eulogize suicide as "right-to-die" or "death-with-dignity." Many respected bioethicists, psychiatrists, psychologists, and social workers no longer believe that mental health professionals have a duty to prevent all suicides. They assert that professionals have a moral duty to attempt to stop only irrational suicides—that is, those they deem impulsive or frivolous. In their opinion, a rational suicide would be that of a person with a terminal illness who should be allowed to choose death before it would otherwise occur.

Demographics suggest that the current trend to rationalize and glamorize suicide will continue to move our national culture in a pro-suicide direction. As the baby-boom generation—people born between 1946 and 1964—advances toward old age and frailty, euthanasia and PAS will become a more acceptable means of coping with the pain and pessimism often associated with the end of life. The United States Centers for Disease Control and Prevention (CDC) reports that there were 31,484 suicides in the country in 2003. This number is twice as high as the number of people who were murder victims. Forty-five percent of all these suicides were committed by men and women over the age of sixty-five. As older Americans turn to one form of suicide or another as the ultimate solution to the perils of aging, society should be cognizant of the lesson it is imparting to the young. The 2003 CDC statistics reveal that among young people between the ages of fifteen and twenty-four, suicide (3,988 victims) is the third largest cause of death. This number has trebled since 1952 and is expected to continue to increase as the nation's senior citizens become more tolerant of suicide.

Suicide in America is as complex an issue as any that this society will probably face in the near future. Few concerns involve constitutional and statutory law, individual and societal rights, generational love, religion and secularism, pain and suffering, compassion and forgiveness, and promised and unfulfilled solutions to the degree that suicide does. In *Current Controversies: Suicide,* authors from across the moral and rationalist divide present their views. With the exception of youth suicide, there is no consensus that the country's growing tolerance of suicide is undesirable. Some secular writers believe that Americans are guaranteed the rights to life, liberty, and death. Some Christians, on the other hand, assert that the sanctity of life supersedes any commonly held legal and political values. Suicide is interpreted through the prism of partisan politics. Republicans and social conservatives are viewed as capitalizing on the death of Terri Schiavo, who for years lived in a persistent vegatative state, to advance their positions on abortion and euthanasia. The Democratic Party is accused of repudiating its progressive roots that hold that the most vulnerable among us should be protected, and of evolving instead into the party that champions the notion that some lives are not worth living. In the end, the only universally held opinion on the matter is that the nation and the medical profession have to do a better job of preventing and studying the underlying causes of teen suicide.

CHAPTER 1

Is Suicide Immoral?

Chapter Preface

Over the past fifteen years, public attitudes on the morality of end-of-life issues have steadily changed. This attitude adjustment, in part, is related to advances in medical technology and to the aging of the baby boomer generation. According to a 2005 Pew Research Center for the People & the Press survey, 60 percent of those polled believe that people have a moral right to end their lives if they suffer from great pain and foresee no opportunity to improve their physical and or mental health condition. This is an increase of 19 percent since 1975 when the poll question was first asked. Much of this attitude change occurred between 1975 and 1990 when those who favored it increased from 41 percent to 55 percent. Since 1990, the number of Americans expressing the moral right to suicide viewpoint increased (5 percent) at a much slower pace.

Interestingly, there are considerable gender and racial differences over the morality of suicide. In situations where there is no hope of improvement, 66 percent of men and 54 percent of women support a right to end one's own life. In racial terms, 62 percent of whites believe people have a moral right to end their lives under such circumstances, compared with just 43 percent of blacks. It is not surprising that viewpoint on these weighty matters is reflective of religious views and/or political persuasion. Forty-two percent of white evangelical Protestants and 40 percent of Catholics believe that an individual suffering from great pain with no hope of improvement has a moral right to suicide, compared to 78 percent of secularists. Moreover, 83 percent of liberal Democrats think people have a moral right to end their lives under these circumstances compared to 41 percent of socially conservative Republicans. Both moderate Republicans and moderate Democrats fall in between with 63 percent and 62 percent, respectively.

While more people have come to agree that an individual has a moral right to suicide over the past three decades, the same is not true on the issue of mercy killing. In 2005, 29 percent of Americans believed that killing a terminally ill spouse was never justified. While mercy killing is still a minority-held view, its adherents have increased 9 percent since 1990. Much of the opposition comes from white evangelical Protestant baby boomers born between 1958 and 1972. On the other end of the spectrum, only 6 percent of Americans believe that mercy killing is always justified.

Palestinian Suicide Bombers Are Immoral {

Robert Tracinski

About the author: *Robert Tracinski is the editor and publisher of* The Intellectual Archivist, *a monthly magazine that analyzes current political, cultural, and philosophic issues from a pro-individualist perspective.*

The West's conflict with Islamic terrorism is more than a "clash of civilizations." It is, at root, a clash between two world views and two moral models, a clash much wider and more important than any political conflict.

Palestinian Self-Sacrifice

I was reminded of this by a brilliant observation in a recent column by [*Washington Post* newspaper columnist] Charles Krauthammer—an observation far more significant than Krauthammer himself seems prepared to recognize. Writing about the way in which Palestinians have consistently rejected every opportunity for statehood, peace, and prosperity, instead choosing constant warfare and destruction, he concludes: "This embrace of victimhood, of martyrdom, of blood and suffering, is the Palestinian disease."

What Krauthammer doesn't realize is that this worship of suffering is the *world's* disease, a very old affliction that has evaded our cultural immune system by disguising itself as a morality. That morality is accepted as uncontroversial in today's world, and you hear it, and probably nod in agreement, whenever someone tells you that *self-sacrifice* is the essence of moral virtue.

But isn't self-sacrifice—or, as Krauthammer puts it, "victimhood, martyrdom, blood and suffering"—the essence of

Robert Tracinski, "The Suicide Bomb Morality," *Real Clear Politics*, June 21, 2006. Reproduced by permission.

the horrific plight the Palestinians have chosen for themselves? And shouldn't this make us question, at its very roots, the morality of self-sacrifice?

The Palestinians show us a society based on sacrifice in its purest, most fanatical form. It is a society built around a single moral model: the suicide bomber, who is lionized on billboards, on television, in popular songs. And this is not just the propaganda of the corrupt Palestinian rulers. One of the delegates elected to the Palestinian parliament in the populist upsurge for [the terrorist group] Hamas [the majority political party] was Umm Nidal, the "mother of martyrs," who has sent three of her sons to kill themselves in terrorist attacks on Israel, proclaiming that their "sacrifice . . . makes me happy."

For the great mass of Palestinians this worship of sacrifice is sincere. By rejecting every chance at peace and coexistence with Israel—breaking every truce and turning down every peace offer—they have lost everything and gained nothing. Taking the suicide bomber as their moral model, the Palestinians seek to emulate his fate: in their lust to destroy Israel, they are willing to accept the utter destruction and collapse of their own society.

Israeli Opposing Moralities

Look to the other side of the security barrier and you see a very different society. While the Palestinians raise their children on visions of blood and murder, the Israelis are largely preoccupied by the business of producing, creating, making a living. Consider, for example, the vast Gaza greenhouses handed over from the departing Israelis to the Palestinians. In the hands of the society that "made the desert bloom," these greenhouses produced millions of dollars' worth of produce. Under Palestinian control, they were looted and their products have literally been left to rot. As with the Cold War examples of East and West Berlin, Gaza and Israel offer side-by-side laboratories for opposing moralities.

American Morality

The contrast to America—a nation founded on the right to "the pursuit of happiness"—is even more vivid. When [the French political thinker] Alexis de Tocqueville visited America in 1832, he reported that the moral doctrine of "self-interest properly understood"—not hedonism, but a version of rational, benevolent self-interest—was "universally accepted": "You hear it as much from the poor as from the rich."

The distinctive model for American culture is not the suicide bomber but the "self-made man": the entrepreneur who achieves prosperity by hard work and ingenuity. Implicitly, we recognize that the proper business of life is not sacrifice but *achievement*. This is the actual code by which most Americans live.

The tragedy is that we don't recognize it.

The West Is Morally Intimidated

We are still too morally intimidated by unquestioned traditions, or by the confused invocation of the "sacrifice" of our courageous soldiers—which fails to recognize that it is an act of the most profound self-interest to resist the rule of tyranny and terror. And so we pay lip service to the nobility of sacrifice.

This lip service undercuts our certainty and moral clarity, not only in dealing with terrorism, but also at home. British columnist Janet Daley, for example, worries that the right hasn't come up with a "morally attractive case for capitalism" despite the fact that "it is free markets that have delivered mass prosperity and personal self-fulfillment on a scale unprecedented in human history." But is this really such a mystery, when everyone denounces "selfishness," so that personal prosperity and "self-fulfillment" are viewed as morally unimportant at best and morally suspect at worst?

Only one prominent intellectual in the last century—Ayn Rand, the great intellectual defender of individualism—has been brave enough to name the moral lesson. Rejecting the morality of sacrifice, she declared that "The purpose of morality is to teach you, not to suffer and die, but to enjoy yourself and live," while in her classic novel *The Fountainhead*, her hero laments that "The world is perishing from an orgy of self-sacrificing." Ayn Rand remains a controversial figure, scoffed at by both left and right. But this phrase, "perishing from an orgy of self-sacrificing"—could there be a better description of the Palestinians' suicide bomb society?

Look at the horrific plight the Palestinians have chosen, and you can observe the real meaning of a culture of self-sacrifice. Look at America, by comparison, and you can see the life-affirming benevolence of a culture of rational self-interest.

The evidence is out there, and its moral lessons are clear—if only we are brave enough to learn from them.

Christians Believe in the Sanctity of Life

Christianity Today

About the author: Christianity Today *magazine provides evangelical thought leaders a sense of community, coherence, and direction through biblical commentary on issues.*

Some critics are calling social conservatives hypocrites for opposing *Roe v. Wade* and siding with the federal government in *Gonzales v. Oregon*, the assisted suicide case heard by the Supreme Court in October [of 2005]. You can't be for states' rights in one case and against them in the other. Or both for and against "judicial activism."

Though we often argue cases using political and legal reasoning, critics need to realize that these are not the central issues for us. We're against Oregon's law because it promotes taking human life, radically demeans personhood, and ultimately and idolatrously deconstructs the image of God that we as humans bear. And we need to be clear about that.

Political Argument

Let's look at the political argument first. Critics point out that Oregon's assisted suicide law was twice endorsed by voters in statewide referendums. When then [U.S.] Attorney General John Ashcroft declared the use of federally controlled substances in assisted suicide a violation of the federal Controlled Substances Act and not a "legitimate medical purpose," he was violating principles of states' rights and democracy, they say.

The *Wall Street Journal* was among the critics. *Roe v. Wade*, it said in an editorial, "substituted the opinion of a handful of jurists for what would have been a contentious, but in the end healthier, open, and democratic debate over where to draw the line on the legality of abortion. . . . A finding for the attorney general in the Oregon case would repeat that mistake on the question of assisted suicide."

But a finding against Oregon would not be a blow against states' rights. As *The Oregonian* associate editor David Reinhard noted, "States' rights doesn't mean a state can take over or ignore an established area of federal regulation." Nor are those of us against Oregon's law necessarily siding with that new conservative Christian bogeyman, "judicial activism."

Transcendent Truth

As important as politics is, though, we need to regularly lift up moral issues involved. Yes, some reply, but isn't it better to speak Washington's indigenous language of power and rights than to speak about transcendent truths that may be dismissed as irrelevant in a pluralistic society? And isn't there a trend to write off "moral disapproval" as not just irrelevant to policy, but also as an unconscionable sign of "animus"?

Yet by speaking only in terms of power and rights—states' rights, the rights of the attorney general, doctors' rights, the right to life—we do a tremendous disservice to justice and to God.

Ultimate Issue Is Justice

When we speak as lawyers in a court of law or as doctors at a medical inquiry, naturally, we must use the language appropriate to the context. But when we speak in our capacity as Christians or as a church, political language can become a liability. As the criticisms above show, people can become confused about what is central. Furthermore, when we fail to mention the real reasons we're against assisted suicide, we are dishonest. We also risk suggesting that our political ideology and our prudential judgments are somehow moral or Christian or even absolutes. As it was for the prophets, for us the ultimate issue is justice, not federalism; idolatry, not "judicial activism."

Maintaining this focus can also remind us that complete victory this side of the kingdom is ever elusive. For instance, if the Supreme Court affirms the Ashcroft Directive—which hinges on the use of federally controlled substances to kill people—Oregon could still rewrite its law without the use of a federally controlled substance. It should go without saying that we would be against that law, too, and that federalism or states' rights or judicial activism has nothing to do with it.

This distinction between our moral foundation and our prudential tactics is crucial in the big picture. The conflagration over the failed Harriet Miers nomination to the [U.S.] Supreme Court illustrated that the conservative coalition is tentative at best. Religious conservatives are not social conservatives, fiscal conservatives, or economic liberals, but we share beliefs that overlap with the others, and we form alliances on various points. Still, on other points, we must stand against these allies and tell them they are wrong. (And when we do so, it should be because they truly are wrong, not because we are aiming to build political capital with another group.)

Human Life Trumps Political and Legal Values

Realists and pragmatists may counter that this isn't how things are done. Better to focus with political allies on "a time to be silent and a time to speak" than on "a time to embrace and a time to refrain". Moralists, prophets, and others who aren't team players win few ears in lawmaking, it is said.

True, in day-to-day politics, give-and-take and forming alliances is the way to gain numbers and get things done. At the same time, we are wise to remember that the issues ultimately at stake are not those the Court is actually debating.

Yet even in this debate, there are signs of transcendence. When Congress enacted the Controlled Substances Act, U.S. Solicitor General Paul Clement told the Supreme Court, "They were concerned about drug abuse, not for its own sake, but for the debilitating effect it has on people's lives, for its tendency to destroy lives." That value on human life trumps any political or legal values we might hold, and it is something we must shout from the housetops.

Voluntary Stopping of Eating and Drinking Raises Moral Issues for Doctors

Lynn A. Jansen

About the author: *Lynn A. Jansen is a senior medical ethicist at John J. Conley Department of Ethics at St. Vincent's Medical Center, Manhattan, New York.*

In response to significant public controversy over the moral and legal permissibility of physician-assisted suicide (PAS), a number of writers have proposed voluntary stopping of eating and drinking (VSED) as an alternative to PAS. Some have claimed that VSED is a practice that "avoids moral controversy altogether." Others, while acknowledging that this practice raises ethical questions for clinicians, have not explored these questions in detail.

The purpose of this paper is not to argue for or against VSED as an acceptable practice for responding to terminal suffering. Instead, the paper calls attention to and discusses some of the ethical complications that surround this practice, complications that have not been adequately addressed in the literature on VSED. Far from avoiding moral controversy altogether, the paper argues that VSED raises very difficult ethical questions. These questions center on the moral responsibility of clinicians who care for the terminally ill as well as the nature and limits of the authority they exercise over them.

VSED

To begin with, VSED must be distinguished from other instances of patient refusal of hydration and nutrition. Sometimes patients cease to eat and drink because they suffer from

Lynn A. Jansen, "No Safe Harbor: The Principle of Complicity and the Practice of Voluntary Stopping of Eating and Drinking," *Journal of Medicine and Philosophy*, vol. 29, 2004, pp. 61–74. © Taylor & Francis Ltd. Reproduced by permission of Taylor & Francis Group and the author. www.taylorandfrancis.com.

a condition that interferes with normal appetite, swallowing, digestion, or absorption of water and essential nutrients. When this occurs, patients do not make an intentional decision to stop eating and drinking. By contrast, VSED occurs when competent patients intentionally refuse to eat and drink (and refuse artificial feedings and hydration) as a means of responding to their suffering and/or gaining more control over their deaths. If a competent patient's decision to engage in VSED is voluntary, his or her physician is morally and legally required to respect it. The physician also may be morally required to provide the patient who engages in VSED with appropriate medication for treating the pain and suffering that can accompany the refusal of hydration and nutrition. Indeed, some writers have suggested that if patients who engage in VSED become delirious or seriously agitated then their physicians should consider initiating terminal sedation to ensure their comfort as they die.

We do not have at present a clear understanding of the boundaries of the concept of suicide.

Notwithstanding its legal permissibility, some clinicians have expressed unease about VSED. They have thought that it will (or could be) used as a method for patients to commit suicide as a way of responding to feelings of powerlessness, social isolation and suffering. For those clinicians who think that suicide is morally wrong participation in this practice may appear to be ethically suspect. It therefore is of some importance to ask, is VSED a method of patient suicide?

Different Types of VSED

The issue is not straightforward. As several writers have pointed out, physicians are required to respect the rights of their terminally ill patients to engage in VSED for the same reasons that they are required to honor a competent patient's rational refusal of a variety of life-prolonging interventions. However, the refusal by patients of life-prolonging interventions—particularly those that are judged to be disproportionately burdensome—is generally *not* considered to be an act of suicide. If continuing to eat and drink becomes intolerable for a patient given his physical condition and his proximity to death, then his participation in VSED may be characterized more accurately not as an act of suicide, but rather as a rational refusal to take disproportionately burdensome steps to keep himself alive.

Even if some instances of VSED are not plausibly described as acts of suicide, it is reasonable to think that others are.

We need, accordingly, to be more precise about different instances of VSED and their relation to suicide. This is complicated by the fact that we do not have at present a clear understanding of the boundaries of the concept of suicide. According to a standard definition, a person commits suicide if she intentionally brings about her own death, others do not coerce her into action, and death is caused by conditions arranged by her for the purpose of bringing about her own death. In light of what was said above, we should add to this that the conditions arranged by the person to bring about her own death are not simply the refusal to take disproportionately burdensome steps to stay alive.

This definition suggests that we need to distinguish broadly between two classes of terminally ill patients. Members of the first class have an irreversible lethal illness and suffer from an underlying physiological condition that is not responsive to standard palliative care. Members of the second class likewise have an irreversible lethal illness, but their physiological suffering can be appropriately managed by standard palliative care. Despite this, these patients still experience psychosocial suffering, which results from their awareness that they will die soon or that they have lost control over their lives.

When terminally ill patients in the first class engage in VSED, then it may not be plausible to characterize their act in terms of suicide. Perhaps they are simply refusing to take disproportionately burdensome steps to keep themselves alive. By contrast, when those in the second class engage in VSED then there is a much stronger case for characterizing it as an instance of suicide. Their refusal of food and fluids follows from an intentional decision to end their lives as a means for alleviating their sense of fear, powerlessness, and social isolation.

The distinction between these two classes of terminally ill patients is, admittedly, quite rough. I do not mean to suggest that it will be easy always to determine when an instance of VSED is a form of suicide. The judgment that a particular patient who is close to death has committed suicide will often be controversial. The distinction between these two classes of terminally ill patients is introduced here merely to underscore a modest, but important, point. *Even if some instances of VSED are not plausibly described as acts of suicide, it is reasonable to think that others are.* This is important, for many physicians believe for both moral and religious reasons that suicide is an impermissible act. The unease that has been expressed about VSED, therefore, can be best understood as the worry that at least some terminally ill patients will use this practice to commit suicide; and that where this is the case or where it is a possibility, physicians should not encourage them to do so.

Physician Complicity in VSED

This unease will not be shared by all. Clinicians who have no moral objections to PAS or voluntary euthanasia are unlikely to have reservations about terminally ill patients committing suicide by voluntarily refusing to eat and drink. But since VSED has been advocated as an alternative to PAS—one that can and should be accepted even by opponents of PAS—it is instructive to consider VSED from the perspective of those who oppose patient suicide.

Consider, then, the issue of physician participation in VSED from the standpoint of a physician who believes that patient suicide, even by terminally ill patients, is morally impermissible. Suppose this physician has a competent terminally ill patient under his care who engages in VSED. The ethical requirements of the physician in this kind of case are clear. While he may attempt to discourage the patient from doing so, he ultimately must honor the patient's decision. He must not intervene and impose enteral and/or intravenous feeding procedures on the patient to keep him alive. The physician also may have a duty to provide whatever palliative measures would be appropriate for alleviating the pain and suffering likely to accompany the refusal of hydration and nutrition.

It is possible that a physician might believe that the wrongness of patient suicide through the practice of VSED would justify overriding the rights of patients to refuse treatment. If so, then this physician's moral beliefs would be in conflict with the settled understanding of the professional duties of a physician. Furthermore, in most European countries, as well as in the United States, physicians have a legal duty to respect the rights of patients to refuse treatment. For these reasons, the claim that physicians must respect the patient's right to refuse food and fluids is, for the most part, common ground among defenders and critics of PAS. It helps explain why some writers have said that VSED can "avoid moral controversy altogether".

Important ethical difficulties arise, however, when physicians find themselves in situations where they must decide whether to take an active role in the decision-making process that may result in a patient engaging in VSED. Here the nature and extent of the physician's participation with the patient's decision raises important ethical questions that have not been confronted by those who have discussed the ethics of this practice.

These questions concern the issue of physician complicity in patient wrongdoing. The issue of complicity arises because, as one writer has put it, "each of us is specially responsible for what *he* does rather than for what other people do." When others are engaging in or planning to engage in wrongdoing, a responsible moral agent will not only consider what she may be able to do to prevent the wrongdoing, but also to what extent she is implicated in the wrongdoing. Sometimes a responsible moral agent will conclude that while there is nothing he can do to prevent a wrongful act, he must take steps to distance himself from it.

The issue of complicity is relevant to medical ethics because physicians, like everyone else, are moral agents. To maintain their moral integrity they must make decisions that are in line with their best moral judgment. It is simply an error to think that physicians can avoid making moral judgments altogether and thereby avoid the issue of complicity. Even if a physician were to decide that she should always defer to the preferences of her patients, this decision itself would rest on a moral judgment about the importance of respecting the preferences of patients. It is also an error to think that physicians should not be too concerned with their own moral integrity. The fact that a physician occupies a professional role does not free her from the responsibilities of being a moral agent. Like others, physicians have a responsibility to avoid participating in wrongful practices.

Hypothetical Examples of Physician Involvement in VSED

To bring the issue of complicity into sharper focus and to relate it to the issues that we are concerned with in this paper, I

33

now shall present two hypothetical cases that illustrate different degrees of physician participation in VSED.

Case 1: Karen is a 63-year old patient with a glioblastoma of the left frontoparietal area [a brain tumor]. She is given Dexamethasone and antiseizure medication to manage her headaches and seizures. These interventions are generally effective, but occasionally Karen experiences focal seizures followed by confusion and severe muscle weakness. These episodes are deeply troubling to her. After careful deliberation with her family members and her minister, Karen tells her physician that she fears losing control of her own life and that she would like him to help her end it. Her physician responds that it is against the law and against his moral conscience for him to assist in her suicide, but he informs her that she has a legal right to stop eating and drinking and to refuse food and fluids. He tells her that if she chooses this route, then he is required by law to respect her decision. Three days later Karen stops eating and drinking. One week later she dies.

In this case Karen's decision to stop eating and drinking may be justified, but it is an error to think that her physician bears no moral responsibility for her decision. By informing her of her legal right to engage in VSED, he collaborates with her in reaching this decision. *If* her decision was morally impermissible, then a case can be made that he too has acted wrongly. The case rests on the idea that it is wrong to assist others in wrongdoing or to advise them to engage in wrongdoing or even to provide them with information that will assist or tempt them to do so. This idea is sometimes referred to as the *principle of complicity* or the principle of cooperation.

Of course, it may be that Karen's decision in case 1 is morally justifiable. If so, and if her physician believed her decision was morally permissible, then he did no wrong in informing her about the option to engage in VSED. The point here is merely that if we accept the principle of complicity then the moral permissibility of the physician's conduct in case 1 turns, in part at least, on the moral character of Karen's decision.

This is a natural error to make ... for it is easy to think that if the decision to engage in VSED is the patient's decision, then the physician is let off the moral hook.

Further ethical considerations bear on case 1. In particular, some may object that merely providing information to patients about a legally protected option is *not* to collaborate with them in pursuing that option. Before turning to these considerations, however, I need to present the second case. This case varies only slightly, but in morally significant ways, from case 1.

Case 2: David suffers from the same underlying condition as Karen. He suffers from the same symptoms and he has received the same treatment. Like Karen, after deliberating with his family and minister, he asks his physician to assist him in terminating his life. David's physician responds that it is against the law and against her moral conscience for her to assist in his suicide, but she informs him that he has a legal right to refuse food and fluids. Sensing David's concern about this option, she reassures him that this can be done with minimal suffering. She informs him that there is mounting evidence that patients who die from lack of hydration and nutrition can die comfortably, so long as adequate pain management is provided. She also reassures him that he should not feel moral guilt about engaging in VSED. She points out that it is his decision to make, not hers; but that she will support his decision either way. Three days later David stops eating and drinking. One week later he dies.

David's decision to stop eating and drinking may or may not be justified, but once again it is an error to think that his physician bears no moral responsibility for his decision. This is even clearer in this case than in case 1, for David's physician not only informs him of the legal option to engage in VSED, but also assuages his worries about the practice. She actively reassures him and comes close to attesting to the ethical acceptability of this option. This amounts to a significantly greater degree of collaboration on the part of the physician. Many clinicians who believe the physician acts permissibly in case 1 will think the physician in case 2 does not.

The key idea, however, is illustrated by both cases, even though it is more vividly illustrated in case 2 than in case 1. The idea is that it is wrong to participate in and/or assist others in committing morally impermissible actions. On the assumption that the physicians in both of the cases presented have moral objections to suicide, they may be making an error in failing to see that by collaborating with their patients on the decision to engage in VSED they are participating in wrongdoing themselves. This is a natural error to make; . . . for it is easy to think that if the decision to engage in VSED is the patient's decision, then the physician is let off the moral hook. Thoughtful attention to the principle of complicity should keep clinicians from committing this error. . . .

Physician Moral Complicity in VSED

In both of the cases showcased above the physician knowingly participates in the patient's decision to stop eating and drinking. Neither physician can claim that he was non-negligently unaware that his patient might decide to engage in VSED. Nor can either physician claim that his actions were sufficiently "distant" from the patient's decision that no issue of material cooperation arises. Indeed, each presents VSED as an option for the patient to consider. Does this amount to complicity in wrongdoing?

Here we must tread carefully. I have been arguing that the ethical acceptability of physician involvement in VSED depends on two factors: (1) the moral permissibility of the patient's decision and (2) the degree to which the physician collaborates with the patient in reaching this decision. In effect, then, I have advanced a conditional argument: *If* patient suicide is morally wrong, and *if* some instances of VSED are instances of patient suicide, then it is wrong for clinicians to participate in these instances of VSED.

Proponents of VSED can rebut this argument by denying the antecedent. They might argue that (in all or most instances) VSED is in fact a morally acceptable practice for responding to suffering at the end of life. However, as I called attention to earlier, much of the interest in VSED stems from the idea that it is a practice that both proponents and critics of PAS can affirm without abandoning their fundamental moral commitments. A defense of VSED that proceeds by arguing that patient suicide is not morally wrong pretty clearly will betray this hopeful idea.

Furthermore, and importantly, even those who believe that VSED is morally permissible ought to be able to concede that some reasonable clinicians think otherwise. In modern pluralistic societies reasonable persons disagree over the permissibility of a range of practices such as abortion, genetic cloning, animal experimentation and capital punishment. It is important to deliberate over the "right" answers to the issues raised by these practices; but in addition we need to consider the degree to which different clinicians can participate in them while remaining faithful to their conscience. If a mistaken conscience can bind, then even those who believe that all or most instances of VSED are morally permissible should be able to understand how clinician participation in this practice could be morally troubling. That is why it is appropriate to discuss the problem of complicity with respect to VSED even if we have not yet resolved the issue of when, and under what conditions, the practice is morally permissible. . . .

Treating patients at the end of life is a morally challenging enterprise. Physicians who participate in this enterprise have the responsibility of reaching reasonable decisions about the moral acceptability of different practices for responding to terminal suffering. In light of this, it is natural and admirable for physicians to search for treatment options for end of life suffering that avoid moral controversy.

Many have defended VSED as such an option. However, as I have tried to make clear in this paper, VSED raises difficult moral questions about the extent to which physicians can permissibly collaborate with moral wrongdoing (or with what they perceive to be moral wrongdoing) as well as the nature and limits of the authority they exercise over terminally ill patients. I have not tried to offer the last words on these difficult questions. Instead, I wanted simply to call attention to them. Perhaps, however, my discussion provides support for a modest, but important, conclusion. While we might wish otherwise, in orchestrating care at the end of life, there is no moral safe harbor.

Suicide Bombers
Are Moral Martyrs

Margaret P. Battin

About the author: *Margaret P. Battin is a distinguished professor of philosophy and adjunct professor of internal medicine, Division of Medical Ethics, at the University of Utah.*

To cite just some of many examples, the Tamil Tigers have pursued a strategy of suicide attacks to pursue separatist aims in Sri Lanka; the Japanese kamikaze units used air and submarine suicide attacks during World War II; on September 11, 2001, al-Qaeda operatives used suicidal airplane crashes to destroy the World Trade Center and other targets in the United States; Palestinian militants have targeted Israeli civilians in tactical terrorist missions labeled *jihad* [holy war], and Iraqi defenders loyal to Saddam Hussein have tried to target U.S. military invaders. Most prolonged in the Palestine/Israel conflict, such missions have typically involved using young people strapped with explosives, dispatched as ordinary pedestrians to outdoor cafés, buses, seaside resorts, university commons, or anywhere civilians could be killed, on what the West called *suicide bombings* but which the militants themselves understood as *martyrdom*. In these remarks, I'd like to explore the deeper conceptual and ethical significance of tactical suicide missions within the context of more general issues about suicide, self-sacrifice, heroism, martyrdom, and other forms of self-caused death. What, exactly, accounts for the heightened moral repugnance with which these missions are viewed, compared to other resistance, military, and guerrilla tactics? Is

Margaret P. Battin, "The Ethics of Self-Sacrifice: What's Wrong with Suicide Bombing?" *Archives of Suicide Research*, vol. 8, 2004. Copyright © International Academy for Suicide Research. Reproduced by permission of Taylor & Francis, Ltd., http//: www.tandf.co.uk/journals and the author.

there adequate moral ground for this heightened repugnance—dubbed with the particularly pejorative label of "suicide"—or is it merely a matter of ideological prejudice?

Global Tactical Suicide Practices

Questions of *tactical* suicide and self-sacrifice arise in many practices around the globe, including situations like deliberate self-starvation in northern Ireland, fatal hunger strikes in Turkey, and self-immolation for reasons of social protest in Vietnam and Japan. Questions of tactical or goal-oriented suicide and self-sacrifice are also relevant to widely debated domestic questions of death and dying in terminal illness, severe disability, and extreme old age as well, where suicide may be undertaken in order to avoid pain, alleviate one's suffering, reduce health care costs, or spare one's family the anguish of watching a difficult death. Indeed, such issues are relevant in a great many contexts, among them literature—for example, in figures from Sophocles' Ajax to Goethe's Werther; philosophy—for example, in accounts from Plato to Hume; in theology, as in writings from Thomas Aquinas to Dietrich Bonhoeffer, and many, many more. The conceptual and ethical issues I wish to explore here about tactical suicide in political contexts, exhibited particularly vividly in the Israel/Palestine conflict, are not primarily questions about military strategy, but at a deeper level issues about the role of the individual in bringing about his or her own death and equality in defending oneself from death.

Cultural Traditions of Suicide

Virtually all major world traditions involve conceptual tension over the issue of self-caused death. In what is known as the Judeo-Christian tradition, suicide comes to be rejected (at least by the time of Augustine) as sinful, but is often conceptually difficult to distinguish from voluntary martyrdom—death accepted and in many cases sought or embraced to attest to one's faith and perhaps to seek salvation. In contrast, the tradition that begins with Hinduism and comes to include Buddhism includes many currents that emphasize release from self and from cycles of birth and rebirth: one seeks *not* to be reborn. Conceptual and moral tension is also evident in accounts of other forms of tactical suicide, for example Japan's use of kamikaze aircraft and submarine attacks towards the end of World War II, or the self-immolation of Buddhist monks and nuns to protest the policies of the Diem government during the Vietnam war. Similarly, current suicide bombing attacks by Palestinian militants and some few Iraqi loyalists must also be understood against a set of cultural and religious backgrounds, including Islam's uncompromising prohibition of suicide as well as its simultaneous embrace of voluntary martyrdom in the defense of the faith. But background cultural traditions are hardly the whole story, and conversance with them does not reveal the full depth of the moral issues— though in the end I think background cultural traditions will play a major role in the explanation of what is wrong.

The Palestinian populace is desperate. Its young people are angry and hopeless.

Psychopathology of Suicide

Scientific theories of suicide beginning with [Emile] Durkheim, [Sigmund] Freud, and other figures at the beginning of the twentieth century variously understand the phenomenon of suicide as the product of specific forms of social organization, or as the product of ubiquitous human traits— for example, the expression of a deep-seated "death wish" or the product of psychopathology, as in depression or other mental illness, and in many other ways. Current research in suicidology further identifies epidemiological patterns of suicide, psychological profiles and traits that are held to characterize heightened suicide risk, and biochemical markers that are associated with suicide. Under contemporary scientific theories that attempt to understand suicidal behavior like self-starvation, self-immolation, and suicide bombing, an adequate account must uncover the psychopathology involved, including that brought about by the oppressed situation of political groups. The Palestinians' turn to suicide bombing, many contemporary analyses suggest, results from the desperate situation of the populace, particularly among young people growing up angry and hopeless, some of them naively idealistic and some of them manipulated for political ends by the group's military strategists.

There is a great deal of truth in these claims. The Palestinian populace is desperate. Its young people are angry and hopeless. The idealism of some is manipulated by military strategists, and families respond to inducements like large cash payments. Just the same, I think there is a great deal more to say about the ethical issues in such practices, and it cannot be assumed that they are simply a matter of psychopathology.

Suicide Bombing Is Immoral

However, suicide bombing also kills the suicide bomber himself or herself. This latter fact is sometimes used to account for the heightened moral repugnance of suicide bombing compared to other forms of political or military aggression: if the loss of life of a suicide-bombing attack is compared to that in a conventional attack of equal force, suicide bombing kills one more: the bomber him or herself. But this crude enumeration of lives lost is unable to account for what is widely perceived as the heightened, indeed aggravated immorality of suicide bombing.

But while this line of thinking points to one of the central characteristics of suicide bombing, its tactical character, it does not without further argument account for the heightened immorality of the practice.

A number of different reasons may be advanced to show that suicide bombing is immoral, and indeed of heightened or, one might say, aggravated immorality.

1. First—and most obviously—tactical suicide bombing kills people. As it has been employed in the Israel/ Palestine conflict, it targets civilians: noncombatants who are killed indiscriminately but in ways designed to maximize public fear and outrage. These include bystanders, bus passengers, people at leisure, people at parties and celebrations, off-duty soldiers, children, and so on, but generally not officials, on-duty military personnel, or other military targets. Clearly, much of the repugnance of the practice is associated with its homicidal character: it is a strategy used to kill people. However, the ways of killing people used by other parties in political conflicts—howitzers, F-16's, bombs lobbed over borders or dropped from the air—also kill people, and while these actions too are considered homicide, they do not seem to arouse the same sort of special moral repugnance that suicide bombing does.

   However, suicide bombing also kills the suicide bomber himself or herself. This latter fact is sometimes used to account for the heightened moral repugnance of suicide bombing compared to other forms of political or military aggression: if the loss of life of a suicide-bombing attack is compared to that in a conventional attack of equal force, suicide bombing kills one more: the bomber him or herself. But this crude enumeration of lives lost is unable to account for what is widely perceived as the heightened, indeed aggravated immorality of suicide bombing.

2. Suicide bombing is often said to be of heightened moral repugnance because it is duplicitous. The suicide bomber can look his or her victims in the eyes, then

violate that act of humanity by blowing them up. Furthermore, the gaze is one-sided: the suicide bomber ar-
rives at the scene disguised, seemingly an everyday pe-
destrian, with the explosive material hidden under
clothes; the purpose too is disguised, and the about-to-
be-victim has no chance to see through the duplicity
involved. The bomber smiles the "smile of joy," *bassamat
al-Farah*, said to symbolize the joy of martyrdom but is
not recognized as such by the westernized victims. When
the first few female suicide bombers acted, the sense of
duplicity was underscored: no one on the target side had
expected women to play such roles.

3. Suicide bombing is also sometimes said to be of heightened moral repugnance because it involves *suicide*, and
suicide is in itself wrong. The fact of suicide thus com-
pounds the wrongness involved in targeting and killing
civilians and other wrong-making features of this practice. But, of course, this is to assume, not prove, that
suicide is wrong, or that it is wrong in this context. The
history of both western and nonwestern thought involves extensive reflection on the question of whether
suicide is wrong in itself, with some thinkers—notably
those associated with monotheistic religious traditions
(like Augustine, Thomas, Muhammad) or with deonto-
logical, principle-based ethical systems (like Kant)—
holding that it is always wrong, while non-western religious systems (especially Hinduism, Buddhism, and
various traditional oral cultures) and somewhat more
consequentialist and situation-relevant ethical thinkers
have typically maintained that while suicide is morally
wrong in some contexts, it is morally permitted or even
obligatory in others (e.g., the Stoics, Hume, Nietzsche).
Thus, the claim that suicide bombing is wrong because
it involves *suicide* does not succeed without challenge.

4. Then, too, it may be argued that suicide bombing is morally problematic because the perpetrator cannot be held accountable; he or she is dead. Of course, many combatants in conventional combat also end up dead, and thus not able to be held accountable; but there is a certain sense in which one's posthumous reputation and memory can be held accountable. It is true that the perpetrator does not have to live with the negative consequences of the deed (in fact, perpetrators are said to believe that they will go to paradise), but the lack of individual accountability hardly seems to account in full for the heightened immorality of the deed. Nor is it clear that suicide bombing would somehow be less problematic if the perpetrator did get away alive; some argue that this would be still worse.

5. Finally, the 'tactical' feature of the suicide may seem to be problematic. While ordinary suicides of depression or remorse or unrequited love may have some dyadic features, aimed as they may be at changing the relationship between the victim and some other person, in tactical suicide bombing the suicide itself *is* the tactic. It does not so clearly exhibit the personal suffering of the person who commits suicide, and it is not just a suicide, but something else. What is an ordinary expression of individual, personal crisis is warped, detractors might say, into a purposive tactic with an immense human cost.

But while this line of thinking points to one of the central characteristics of suicide bombing, its tactical character, it does not without further argument account for the heightened immorality of the practice.

Suicide Bombing Is Amoral

A further line of thinking about the moral issues in suicide bombing does not try to establish its immorality directly, but challenges the notion that such suicides are voluntary, rational acts for which direct ethical assessment is appropriate. This line of thinking construes suicide not so much as *wrong*, but as *sick*: in keeping with contemporary clinical understandings of suicide and suicidal behavior, it sees suicide as pathological. It is thus not subject to moral assessment in ordinary terms; it is essentially amoral, to be condemned because it kills individuals (and the bomber) but not an appropriate subject for blame.

They are [seen as] martyrs, not suicides; their actions are heroic, their self-sacrifice noble and supreme, supported by interpretations of the Qu'ran and Islamic history.

This line of thought is patently anemic. While there is truth in it too and while many of the suicide bombers are surely under intense psychological pressures, are subject to depression, have other mental illnesses, are forced into it in ways that violate autonomy, and so on, it is clear from accounts the bombers have left, videotapes they have made, notes they have written, and observations by others that their choice to engage in this activity was largely voluntary in a robust sense. True, some of those who have acted were still virtually children. But the same cannot be said of, for example, the pilots who trained for the suicide bombing of the Trade Centers, the driver of the van loaded with explosives that drove into the U.S. Embassy in Beirut in 1983, or the Palestinians who schooled themselves long in advance for suicide attacks and competed to be chosen. Nor do external incentives like large payments to surviving family necessarily play a choice-compromising role. What evidence there is suggests that the choices of the suicide bombers have often—though certainly not in every case—been precisely that—choices—and hence appropriate targets for moral assessment. Unlike some (but not all) ordinary suicides, they do not appear to be the product primarily of mental illness; to suggest that suicide bombing is *amoral* rather than *immoral* would be to fail to see one of the central characteristics of this act. Suicide bombing involves electing to die for a cause. As Fathi Shikaki, the spiritual leader of Islamic Jihad who was assassinated in Malta in 1995 had told reporters, he didn't personally choose suicide bombers: "Some of the youths insist that they want to lead a suicide operation— perhaps because they are influenced by the teachings of Islamic Jihad. My orders are to persuade them not to go, to test them. If they still insist they are chosen."

Suicide Bombing Is Moral

Suicide bombing is seen as immoral, and indeed of heightened moral repugnance, by the side that is attacked or has been scheduled to be attacked—Israelis and Americans, as well as many others in the industrially developed, traditionally Judaeo-Christian nations. However, in the areas and nations from which the practice emanates, suicide bombers are seen as morally exemplary agents. They are martyrs, not suicides; their actions are heroic, their self-sacrifice noble and supreme, supported by interpretations of the Qu'ran and Islamic history that date back to at least the seventh century Battle of Karbala. While it is true that the Qu'ran itself implies that suicide is prohibited and the autobiography of Muhammad clearly rejects it, martyrdom and self-sacrifice in defense of Islam are just as clearly celebrated. To the extent that what the west calls suicide bombers are viewed as martyrs by the Islamic Middle East, they are admired, emulated, venerated.

Just as there is more to say about the rejection of suicide by Christianity and to a large extent by Judaism, while at the same time both traditions accept [and] celebrate martyrdom and self-sacrifice; there is more to say about these issues in the context of Islam as well. Clearly, the line between suicide and martyrdom is not drawn in quite the same place in these traditions. Contemporary vocabularies used to discuss these issues—vocabularies, especially scientific ones, for the analysis of suicide, and vocabularies, especially religious ones, for the celebration of martyrdom—tend to obscure these distinctions. But I want to look at a somewhat different issue in trying to tease out what, at least from the point of view of the west, accounts for the heightened moral repugnance of suicide bombing, and what may well account (though I am a good deal less sure about this) for the heightened moral esteem it earns within some factions within Islam.

Suicide Bombing Is an Issue of Fairness

I think the central feature of suicide bombing, in al-Qaeda attacks on the World Trade Center, in Iraqi loyalist attacks on U.S. soldiers, and especially in the attacks of Palestinian militants disguised as pedestrians crossing into Israel, has to do with the apparent violations of tacit presumptions of equality in mortal combat, including war and other forms of combat and aggression. It is, at root, an issue of fairness, one with disturbing implications.

Consider a variety of adages that serve to regulate individual behavior in aggression and combat: "Don't hit a man when he's down." "Don't stab someone in the back." Adages of this sort serve to promote relatively equal circumstances in fighting: you may hit another only when he is "up," that is, standing and not already seriously injured, and thus still in a position to hit you. Similarly, the second adage directs, you may stab a person only when he is facing you, hence able to see what's coming and thus able to prepare for and return the blow; it would be unfair to take advantage of a person by killing him unannounced and from behind, without fair warning. I think adages such as these operate, albeit usually tacitly, in much of our thinking about fighting, combat, aggression, and war. What the use of suicide bombing does is to violate this tacit assumption of equality in combat: suicide bombing confers unfair advantage. The party that employs suicide bombing has a weapon—the stealth and ability to penetrate invisibly into target situations—the other side doesn't. It can generate terror of a distinctive sort, possible precisely because of the tactic's capacity for intimate, unnoticed infiltration. It hits when someone is down, or at least defenseless; it stabs from behind, unexpected, unseen.

Even if the Palestinians have a weapon the Israelis don't—namely, suicide bombing—the Israelis have many, many weapons the Palestinians don't: tanks, F-16's, and . . . nuclear weapons.

This argument may seem utterly facile in the context of the Israel/Palestine conflict. Unfair advantage? Even if the Palestinians have a weapon the Israelis don't—namely, suicide bombing—the Israelis have many, many weapons the Palestinians don't: tanks, F-16's, and, although they haven't used them yet, nuclear weapons. In contrast, the Palestinians, inhabitants of a controlled and occupied zone, have virtually no advanced military hardware at all. To suggest that what is central to the issue of suicide bombing is the notion of unfair advantage may seem insensitive, absurd, or worse.

However, what constitutes an "unfair advantage" is not merely a question of what weapons are currently available, but what one side or the other *could* use. The Palestinians do have the weapon in question, the tactic of suicide bombing—a tactic that, compared to other forms of political resistance, seems to be efficient, effective, and to maximize public notice—and the Israelis do not. However, this is not to say that the Israelis could not use such a tactic and thus, so to speak, even the score. Of course, it could be argued that the Israelis would be controlled in a way that prevents the acquisition of this advantage-conferring weapon, suicide bombing, if for instance international codes of war were to prohibit such tactics, just as the Palestinians are controlled in a way that prevents the acquisition of another set of advantage-conferring weapons, namely tanks, fighter jets, and the like; but while the codes of war prohibit commanders from sending soldiers on clearly suicidal missions, they do not prohibit soldiers from volunteering for high risk missions.

But there is I think a much more interesting argument about the violation of the presumption of equality in such situations. This issue can be perhaps best explored by asking what sort of response to tactical suicide is justifiable, either by individuals or governments. Could, or should, the Israelis, the Americans, and the industrialized west that is the target of *jihad* actions adopt the same sorts of tactics in return? After all, these tactics have been visible and effective in achieving much of the Palestinian aims, with, as is often pointed out, comparatively little loss of life compared to conventional military forms of conflict resolution; they have been described as "the Palestinian H-bomb". The question is not just whether such strategies could happen in other parts of the world as well, either occasionally or as a routine method of pursuing particular political agendas, but whether they should. To be sure, Israel has used a tactic of stealth-based assassinations of Hamas leaders and others believed responsible for the Palestinian uprising and suicide bombings, but these have been actions largely targeted at military figures, not bystander civilians. Americans killed hundred of thousands of fleeing Iraqis during the first Gulf War; these are repugnant actions outside the realm of what is understood as permissible in war. Israelis, Americans, Europeans, and others have all sent their soldiers, sailors, pilots, and other combatants on missions from which there was only miniscule chance that they would return. But neither Israel nor the U.S. nor the Europeans have used suicide bombings or other forms of deliberately tactical suicide, as if there were something distinctively wrong with the deliberate use of *suicide*, somehow more problematic, more wrong than the other ugly actions of war.

Views of Suicide Bombings Are Perceptional

But it is precisely here that the answer about what accounts for perceptions that suicide bombing is of heightened moral repugnance begins to emerge. It is not that the Israelis and the industrialized west do not use such tactics; it is that they *cannot* use them. This, I venture to suggest, is because the long cultural traditions of what has been called Judaeo-Christianity not only revile suicide, but draw the line between suicide and martyrdom in a way that would preclude suicide bombing of the sort employed by the Palestinians and others. It is not that the west does not have this weapon; rather it cannot have it and cannot use it, because its cultural underpinnings provide no respect for it at all. It is, in a deep sense, unthinkable for the west. That is not to say that there might not be some volunteers who would be prepared to sacrifice themselves in this way for a cause they thought worthy, but that there would be little or no cultural support for suicide-based action at all. It could not be conducted as a routine strategy, it could not be counted on for a supply of willing volunteers, and it would not receive the elaborate sorts of social support, including adulation and financial reward, that Palestinian martyrs enjoy.

I think this is at least what makes the Palestinian use of tactical suicide so repugnant to the west. Palestinians can do this with eagerness and seeming ease; but the west cannot respond by flying its airplanes into buildings or sending young volunteers strapped with explosives into Palestinian markets, buses, or cafés. This is a moral inhibition, not a technical one, but a very real one nonetheless.

Suicide bombing, thus, exposes what the west experiences as a weakness in the face of an unfair advantage—"they" can fight in a way "we" cannot. The real issue is whether the use of tactical suicide is indeed morally repugnant, and should be used by neither side in any conflict, or whether its moral legitimacy in combat and war is a function of background cultural ideology: alright for "them," not alright for "us." This is why, I think, the west labels this practice "suicide" (one of the west's most negative, completely pejorative terms), why it refuses to see these actions as defensible cases of martyrdom, and why in general it does not try to think through the morality of the practice, but rejects it out of hand. Clearly, a practice that involves killing is repugnant in that fact alone, but whether it is a practice of heightened, aggravated immorality is the issue that remains to be further explored.

Individual Rights Come Before Religion

Thomas A. Bowden

About the author*: Thomas A. Bowden is a writer for the Ayn Rand Institute in Irvine, California. The institute promotes Objectivism, the philosophy of Ayn Rand. Bowden is also a practicing attorney in Baltimore, Maryland.*

Since 1997 Oregon physicians have been permitted by statute to help their patients commit suicide. On Tuesday [January 17, 2006], the [United States] Supreme Court upheld this controversial law, reaching the right result for the wrong reasons. By basing its decision on legal technicalities, the Court managed to avoid addressing the real issue: an individual's unconditional right to commit suicide.

The Oregon law [The Oregon Death With Dignity Act] permits a doctor to prescribe a lethal dose of drugs to a mentally competent, terminally ill patient who makes written and oral requests, consults two physicians, and endures a mandatory waiting period. The patient's relatives and doctors are powerless to engage in legalized "mercy killing," as they cannot apply on the patient's behalf, and the patient himself administers the lethal dose.

U.S. Supreme Court Decision

In 2001, [U.S.] Attorney General John Ashcroft decreed that any doctor prescribing such a dose would violate federal law against dispensing controlled dangerous substances without a "legitimate medical purpose." Consequently, the case reached the Supreme Court as a technical debate between federal and state governments over which one should regulate the practice of medicine. On Tuesday the Court ruled that the state of Oregon could permit assisted suicide, despite the federal law.

But who was missing from that debate? The individual patients whose lives were at stake.

If you have a duty to go on living, despite your better judgment, then your life does not belong to you, and you exist by permission, not by right.

What the Supreme Court should have done was bypass legal technicalities and revisit its 1997 decision in *Washington v. Glucksberg*, which held that individuals have no constitutionally protected right of suicide, and hence no right to obtain assistance in that act.

What the courts must grasp, if they are ever to resolve the battle over assisted suicide once and for all, is that there is no rational, secular basis upon which the government can properly prevent any individual from choosing to end his own life. When religious conservatives use secular laws to enforce their idea of God's will, they threaten the central principle on which America was founded.

Reasons Why Individuals Have a Right

The Declaration of Independence proclaimed, for the first time in the history of nations, that each person exists as an end in himself. This basic truth—which finds political expression in the right to life, liberty, and the pursuit of happiness—means, in practical terms, that you need no one's permission to live, and that no one may forcibly obstruct your efforts to achieve your own personal happiness.

But what if happiness becomes impossible to attain? What if a dread disease, or some other calamity, drains all joy from life, leaving only misery and suffering? The right to life includes and implies the right to commit suicide. To hold otherwise—to declare that society must give you permission to kill yourself—is to contradict the right to life at its root. If you have a duty to go on living, despite your better judgment, then your life does not belong to you, and you exist by permission, not by right.

For these reasons, each individual has the right to decide the hour of his death and to implement that solemn decision as best he can. The choice is his because the life is his. And if a doctor is willing to assist in the suicide, based on an objective assessment of his patient's mental and physical state, the law should not stand in his way.

Problems with "Playing God"

Religious conservatives' outrage at the Oregon law stems from the belief that human life is a gift from the Lord, who puts us here on earth to carry out His will. Thus, the very idea of suicide is anathema, because one who "plays God" by causing his own death, or assisting in the death of another, insults his Maker and invites eternal damnation, not to mention divine retribution against the decadent society that permits such sinful behavior.

If George W. Bush were to contract a terminal disease, he would have a legal right to regard his own God's will as paramount, and to instruct his doctor to stand by and let him suffer, just as long as his body and mind could endure the agony, until the last bitter paroxysm carried him to the grave. But the Bush administration has no right to force such mindless, medieval misery upon doctors and patients who refuse to regard their precious lives as playthings of a cruel God.

Conservatives crave to inject religion into the bloodstream of American law, thereby assisting in our own national suicide. However, they cannot succeed without the Supreme Court's consent. Sooner or later, the Court must confront the main issue, and decide whether an individual's right to life includes the right to commit suicide.

Catholic Morality Allows Withholding Artificial Nutrition and Hydration

James F. Drane

About the author: *James F. Drane, Ph.D., emeritus professor of clinical bioethics, founded the Bioethics Institute at Edinboro University of Pennsylvania.*

M odern cultures in developed nations are currently in the midst of a very serious debate about how to handle death and dying. People are trying to decide how to help other people to die. Many approach the issue as if it were a new problem, and try to solve the problem by making suicide and euthanasia legal rights.

The debate is usually centered on rare and tragic cases. In the face of particularly difficult dying situations, some secular persons in the U.S. and Europe ask, "Whose life is it anyway?" The answer to that question is obvious and so the debate about how to handle death and dying becomes a matter of what the individual person wants. Freedom, in the sense of individual autonomy, gradually is becoming the only value. Advocates for change in the law claim a "right to die" in the sense of an individual legal right to be assisted in suicide or euthanasia.

The in-place system for making new laws in many nations today reflects neither a deep respect for the social nature of human beings nor for ideal democratic traditions. Rarely do the poor, the undereducated, the politically marginalized citizens have a chance to voice their concerns about proposed legislation in an effective way. They do not have access to the legislators. They cannot hire lobbyists. They do not contribute to political campaigns. But they do worry about being forced into suicide or euthanasia. Poor women, the elderly, the poor who are sick and alone, poor blacks and Latinos and Asians, these groups do not have a role in the debate, but they have everything to lose if nations move to legislate rights to suicide and euthanasia.

In predominantly Catholic cultures, besides the value of individual freedom, what is best for a community is recognized as a major value in creating new legislation. Nations or states influenced by Catholic culture inherit from history a sound and reasonable religious perspective on the meaning of life and death. Such a perspective is critical when individuals or societies face the problem of how to legislate the care of fellow human beings approaching death. Without a religious perspective, death and dying lose their meaning. "They shoot horses, don't they?" is a line that captures the absence of any meaning of death and its tragic consequences.

The first big lesson from history is that people have always helped other people to die.

I want to look back to moral teachings deeply embedded in Catholic tradition in order to take advantage of already developed moral insights. Death and dying today are more and more influenced by medical technologies which can mercilessly extend the dying process. Because dying takes place so often in high-tech medical settings, death is most often dependent upon a decision to withhold the next possible intervention or withdraw a technology that is burdensome. Making such decisions ethically depends upon prudent employment of certain concepts, categories and distinctions which incorporate moral wisdom developed over the centuries.

Catholic Moral Theology

The first big lesson from history is that people have always helped other people to die. Modern doctors tend not to consider this when they set out to create their "new" solutions. Modern doctors, for example, are well educated, but their education pays little attention to history and no attention to theology. They are trained to see medicine as the use of interventions to cure disease and to prolong life. Until very recently, they received little or no training in the different ways of helping people to die.

Too many patients today die at the end of a string of aggressive and intrusive interventions, attached to all kinds of technologies, isolated, alone, and all too often in severe pain. Their deaths speak volumes about the need for an ethics of medical technology. These shocking high-tech deaths fuel a crusade in the U.S. to solve death-and-dying problems by letting patients kill themselves or by demanding that doctors kill them.

Historically, doctors and nurses felt obliged to help dying patients to control the pain and suffering. Doctors and nurses were focused not just on the physical pain, but the emotional, social, and spiritual suffering as well. In Catholic cultures, doctors and nurses didn't say to dying patients, "There's nothing more I can do," and walk away. They stayed with patients who were dying. Their place was at the bedside of a dying patient. Their obligation was first to avoid applying futile treatments to a terminal disease, then to reassure patients that their pain and suffering would be relieved, that they would retain some sense of control, and that they would not be left alone. The hospice movement pulled these practices together into a new medical program.

What history and Catholic moral theology can contribute to questions about the moral limits for medical technology is direction about when to discontinue technologies aimed at curing and when to shift to caring in the sense of providing relief of pain and suffering. Medical professionals familiar with contemporary bioethics and Catholic moral theology until recently knew when and for what reasons life-sustaining treatments may be discontinued or refused, withdrawn or withheld. They knew who can make the decisions and how to determine a right decision. Suddenly this historical moral agreement is being challenged.

Historical medical codes are clear about the necessity of withholding or withdrawing futile and ineffective treatments. And historical Catholic moral teachings provide guidelines for determining when even a possibly effective medical treatment can legitimately be refused in order to let a person die. The basic moral theological guideline requires a balancing of benefit and harm. And the natural law tradition shows how to do the balancing and how to identify harm.

Spanish Catholic Moral Theologians

Sixteenth- and seventeenth-century Spanish moral theologians, from careful and prudential consideration of dying situations, fashioned a simple, sensible and convincing moral guideline: anything which burdens the patient, or is unbeneficial, or causes harm (pain, cost, shame, repugnance, inconvenience and so forth) can serve as the justification for refusing even effective life-sustaining medical interventions. Medical professionals can respect patient or surrogate refusals, and can withhold or withdraw any treatment which the patient or patient's surrogate decides is burdensome, unbeneficial, or harmful.

Nothing in historical expressions of Catholic moral theology could justify continuing to do everything possible to keep a person alive.

This sensible, reasonable, convincing ethical tradition presupposes that life is a basic good, but not an absolute good.

This means that we have to work to preserve life, but everything possible need not and should not be required to preserve life. Both moral theology and medical history support the tradition of helping people to die, not by intentionally killing them but by withdrawing and withholding even life-saving supports when they are burdensome, harmful, or unbeneficial. After treatment is stopped, the focus of medical help is on the many expressions of caring, especially on pain relief.

What drives the efforts to make suicide and euthanasia legal in contemporary societies is experience with a family member's death when the traditional wisdom of stopping interventions at some point was ignored. Consequently, a dying family member winds up being tortured with interventions that either provide no benefit to the person or provide more burden than benefit. The crusade to legalize physician-assisted suicide in the developed world is driven by (1) fear of "high-tech" dying, (2) overemphasis on patient autonomy, (3) worry that dying will ruin a family economically, and (4) repugnance caused by watching a loved one's dying prolonged by technologies like artificial nutrition and hydration which are not withheld or withdrawn.

Nothing in historical expressions of Catholic moral theology could justify continuing to do everything possible to keep a person alive. Life is precious and sacred in Catholic tradition, but human beings simply cannot do everything possible to preserve life. Could anyone imagine being obliged to do everything possible to keep someone alive? Doing everything possible would prolong the dying process, torture the dying patient, and exhaust scarce medical resources, thereby removing basic treatments for the poor and vaccines for needy children. Sometimes basic goods have to be weighed, and one has to be preferred over another.

Doing everything possible to sustain life is economically impossible and would undermine any healthcare system. For

Christians it would also be a major public scandal. Christianity teaches that afterlife is a reality and Christian believers live their lives in anticipation of eternal life in the presence of God. Doing everything possible to sustain this worldly life would publicly contradict a basic belief. If unlimited effort is placed on sustaining this life, then this life is all-important. The idea of an eternal life later would be contradicted by the total commitment of energy and resources to extending this life.

Civil and Canon Law Support Relief from Pain

Historically, doctors always have helped people to die. In Catholic culture, help comes in the form of respect for patient decisions to refuse what is burdensome or harmful or not sufficiently beneficial. Once medical interventions are withdrawn, then providing care in the form of relief for pain and suffering becomes the medical objective. This is what Catholic moral theology has taught for centuries. It remains one of the cornerstones of Catholic bioethics.

May physicians provide relief of pain and suffering even when the pain-relieving drugs may possibly disrupt cardiopulmonary function and hasten the dying process? The Catholic moral tradition responds affirmatively. The act of relieving pain is a good act. The intention is to help and not to kill or harm the patient. The possible bad consequence of disrupting cardiopulmonary function is outweighed by the good effect of pain relief for dying patients. And the pain relief is not provided by the patient's death. This is traditional Catholic moral theology. It is called the "double-effect principle." The intention not to kill is a critical element in this theological teaching because intention to kill would morally undermine even the best of acts. This moral teaching is accepted in both civil and ecclesiastical law. It is reflected in the bioethics policies of Catholic hospitals and healthcare institutions. Why? Because it makes good common sense. It is a reasonable response to the reality of life when life enters the dying process. It is based on what is called natural law. . . .

The Pope Overturns Traditional Catholic Morality

No one . . . expected the pope himself to come out publicly and argue for overturning a centuries-old and rationally respectable moral teaching, which permitted the removal of any medical technology when it no longer provides sufficient benefit to the patient as person. Historically, a long list of distinguished theologians had approved even a patient's refusal of naturally ingestible food and drink if either or both were experienced as too burdensome. Then suddenly, on March 20, 2004, Pope John Paul II gave a talk at an international conference organized by the Vatican for persons working in Catholic healthcare. In his talk, Pope John Paul II declared that medically administered nutrition and hydration is "morally obligatory" and withdrawing feeding tubes constitutes "euthanasia by omission." His declaration contradicted centuries-old Catholic moral teachings. It also flew in the face of a long string of U.S. legal decisions, all of which upheld the definition of technological nutrition and hydration as a medical treatment, that therefore was neither morally *ordinary* nor ethically obligatory.

John Paul II says that "The administration of food and water, even when provided by artificial means, always represents a *natural* means of preserving life not a medical act". For John Paul II, it is the objective reality of the technology which constitutes its moral obligatoriness rather than any benefit that it brings to the patient as person. This claim is contradicted by decisions in every U.S. court case having to do with [artificial nutrition and hydration] (ANH) including the Supreme Court decision in the Nancy Cruzan case. Judges of every political stripe, after careful consideration of relevant medical data, concluded that the only reasonable way of understanding ANH is as a medical technology and not as *natural feeding* or a *natural means of preserving life.*

In the pope's talk . . . the meaning of "benefit to the patient" is reduced to "sustaining life"—even though the patient has no awareness or appreciation of the fact. This is a watershed change.

The pope's talk literally stunned mainline Catholic theologians and Catholic healthcare administrators. . . . The pope abandoned the traditional teaching that such technology must be freely chosen and benefit the patient as person. According to the pope, ANH is *ordinary* (morally obligatory) as long as it carries out its medical function, e.g. "providing nourishment to the patient and alleviation of suffering." The idea of ANH providing alleviation of suffering contradicts a mountain of medical evidence. In many cases, it does just the opposite. And the idea that ANH is morally obligatory as long as or insofar as it provides nourishment, assigns the term *ordinary* (obligatory) to a particular technology without consideration of its effect on the patient as person.

In the pope's talk, the focus was on patients in a persistent vegetative state [(PVS)]. Certainly the ANH technology offers hope of sustaining life for such patients. But, after years in a PVS and without medical hope of recovering any of the lost personal functionings, the nutrition and hydration does not benefit the patient as a person. Rather, it merely extends the vegetative life of the patient. In the pope's talk . . . , the meaning of "benefit to the patient" is reduced to "sustaining life"— even though the patient has no awareness or appreciation of the fact. This is a watershed change.

In the centuries-old Catholic moral tradition, a treatment is obligatory or optional, *ordinary* or *extraordinary*, depending upon its influence on the person and its evaluation by the patient or the patient surrogates. Now, according to the pope, the moral status of artificial nutrition and hydration no longer depends upon the technology's influence on the overall condition of the patient. Moral appropriateness is reduced to the technology's mechanical effects. The pope, it seems, is comparing the situation of a PVS patient in such a state at the end of life with an emerging fetus at the beginning of life, which is also human existence but without the higher personal functions. Perhaps, for consistency's sake, both are assigned absolute value. Life at either end, for whatever reason, no matter what the conditions, can never be let to die. No matter what the situation or context or level of functioning, everything possible must be done to preserve the human life. . . .

In the U.S., the pope's statement appeared at a time when the people of Florida rejected an effort by Gov. [Jeb] Bush to do exactly what the pope argued for. If birth control teachings have caused damage to the authority of church teachings, this latest papal teaching on forced continuation of medical technology in PVS is likely to add even more damage. The pope's teachings on birth control are not convincing to married people, and now his teaching on artificial nutrition and hydration for patients in PVS will be equally unconvincing. His arguments, I believe, will be considered unconvincing to bioethicists and theologians, as well as to ordinary thinking persons. In Catholic natural law—based ethics or moral theology, without convincing reasoning there is no moral authority. Since the pope's statements are not based on scripture, they have to be supported by sound reasoning to have merit. As was the case with Paul VI on the issue of birth control, this pope, in his final years in office, left behind big problems to be faced by future church administrations.

CHAPTER 2

What Are the Causes of Suicide?

Chapter Preface

Suicide is a serious public health problem that affects not only the victim and his or her surviving family and friends, but also the community at large. According to the United States Centers for Disease Control and Prevention (CDC) *National Vital Statistics Reports* (April 2006), in 2003 intentional self-harm or suicide was the eleventh leading cause of death in the nation, with 31,484 victims. There is no simple answer to why some people decide to take their own lives: Unfortunately suicides result from complex interactions among biological, psychological, social, and environmental factors.

Although youth suicides garner much public and medical attention, it is nevertheless true that suicide rates increase with age and are very high among those sixty-five and older. The U.S. Department of Health and Human Services (DHHS), in fact, reported that even though older Americans account for 13 percent of the population, they account for 18 percent of all suicide deaths in 2000. Many elderly people decide to kill themselves with firearms. In 2006, the CDC reported that of the 30,136 persons who died from firearm injuries, firearm suicide accounted for 56 percent in 2003. Forty-six percent of these firearm suicides were committed by individuals sixty-five and older.

Depression is the most common condition associated with suicide in older adults. This form of mental illness is widely under-recognized and undertreated. According to the DHHS, 75 percent of older adults were seen by their physicians a few weeks prior to their suicide attempt and diagnosed with their first episode of depression. The *Archives of General Psychiatry* reports that elderly persons with depression have poor chances of full recovery because most of them remain untreated. Ironically, depression is highly treatable with antidepressant medication, psychotherapy, exercise, social activity or combinations of these treatments. However, seniors may feel that depression is associated with aging or does not merit a doctor's attention. Depression often co-occurs with other serious illnesses such as heart disease, stroke, diabetes, cancer, and Parkinson's disease. In addition, advancing age is often accompanied by loss of key social support systems due to the death of a spouse or siblings, retirement, and/or relocation of residence. To lower the rate of senior suicide, the National Institute of Mental Health is working with primary care clinics across the country to improve recognition and treatment of depression and suicidal symptoms in elderly patients.

Attempted Suicide Can Be a Lucrative Economic Decision

Charles Duhigg

About the author*: Charles Duhigg is a staff writer with the* Los Angeles Times, *where he has pursued investigative features on outdoor recreation and land use and contributed to Iraq coverage from the Baghdad bureau.*

When Kirk Jones jumped over the guardrail at Niagara Falls last week and fell 180 feet alongside 150,000 gallons per second of rushing water, traditional explanations for his leap were plentiful. Jones' parents said he had lost his job and was depressed. A suicide expert pointed out the appeal of dramatic farewells. And everyone called the jump suicidal: Jones is the first person to survive a Niagara fall without safety gear.

But when it later came out that Jones had boasted to a friend, "If I go over and I live, I am going to make some money," it was time to call in the economists.

Jones is now negotiating with tabloids to sell his story for thousands of dollars. His case, however, will complicate a debate that is roiling suicidology, one that pits economists against psychiatrists over a basic question: Is suicide a rational decision?

Economic Theory and Suicide

This controversy began in 1974 when two Princeton economists created a model to forecast suicidal decisions. Admittedly, the economists wrote, some suicidal behavior is purely irrational. But evidence suggests that economic theory explains some suicides. The economists proposed that the value of a life might be calculated the same way we value companies: Measure all the happiness a life might contain, discount it by the cost of achieving that happiness, and if the net present *joie de vivre* is less than zero, suicide is a viable option.

The economics of suicide were largely ignored in the ensuing decades. But last year Dave Marcotte, a professor of public policy at the University of Maryland, Baltimore County, pushed the field forward when he wondered what happens to people like Jones who attempt, but do not achieve, suicide. There are about 20 attempts for every successful suicide. (Approximately 2.9 percent of the U.S. population has attempted suicide—1,760 attempts per day.)

Previous studies had demonstrated that as personal incomes rise, the propensity for suicide falls (presumably, money does buy *some* happiness). Marcotte's insight was that individuals contemplating suicide do not just choose between life and death. Rather, they choose between three alternatives: life, death, and the gray area of unsuccessful suicide, which may be negative (expensive injury and permanent disability) or positive (a "cry for help" that elicits attention).

The resulting formula contains a somewhat paradoxical conclusion: Attempting suicide can be a rational choice, but only if there is a high likelihood it will cause the attempter's life to significantly improve.

It is difficult to find free medical care when you are sad, but once you try to kill yourself, it's forced on you.

Marcotte couldn't test the relative "life improvement" of successful suicides—since they were, of course, dead—but he could study those who had failed at suicide to determine if their lives improved after the attempt. The results are surprising. Marcotte's study found that after people attempt suicide and fail, their incomes increase by an average of 20.6 percent compared to peers who seriously contemplate suicide but never make an attempt. In fact, the more serious the attempt, the larger the boost—"hard-suicide" attempts, in which luck is the only reason the attempts fail, are associated with a 36.3 percent increase in income. (The presence of nonattempters as a control group suggests the suicide effort is the root cause of the boost.)

Why Is Suicide Profitable?

Why should suicide be an economic boon? Once you attempt suicide you suddenly have access to lots of resources—medical care, psychiatric attention, familial love and concern—that were previously expensive or unavailable. Doubters may ask why the depressed don't seek out resources earlier. But studies have demonstrated that psychological and familial resources become "cheaper" after a suicide attempt: It is difficult to find free medical care when you are sad, but once you try to kill yourself, it's forced on you.

Suddenly the calculus of suicide has become even more complicated. Now attempting suicide seems a rational choice, as long as the attempt isn't too successful. But this conclusion alarms suicidologists: Treating suicide as a logical act runs counter to everything they have been advocating for the past 40 years.

The suicide-prevention movement of the 1960s was founded upon the idea of "suicide crisis moments"—relatively brief periods when "psychological pain and mental illness causes irrational thoughts, which are treatable and temporary," explained Dr. David Rudd, president of the American Association of Suicidology. This idea is the basis of suicide hotlines, which studies prove are effective in saving lives. Suicidology suggests that most failed suicide attempts are not caused by permanent mental illness. Rather, they are the products of momentary lapses in reason. Once the crisis moment is resolved through intervention and care, suicidal instincts pass and would-be attempters go on to fruitful and healthy lives. (Many economists and suicidologists agree that *multiple* suicide attempts and successful suicides are often products of long-standing mental illnesses.)

Constructing suicide as a momentary loss of reason is vitally important to the suicide-prevention movement because it suggests that men and women who have attempted self-murder should be allowed to shrug off social stigmas. If suicidal instincts are just momentary delusions, they are easily explained and dismissed. The suicide-prevention movement fears that if suicide is deemed the rational product of someone's mind, we may feel justified in suspecting that mind forever.

But by objecting to rational explanations of suicide, the suicidology community may be undermining its own cause. Although suicide attempts cost the nation more than $3 billion per year, and suicides claim more American lives than homicides, suicide prevention is hampered by scarce resources. Ultimately, say mental health advocates, legislators don't like to fund suicide prevention because they believe that suicidal people must be crazy, and crazy people don't really want help. Perhaps if suicide were considered a rational and combatable disease, like skin cancer or high cholesterol, we might see well funded educational campaigns similar to those for more socially acceptable ailments.

Gun Availability Can Lead to Suicide

David Hemenway

About the author: *Dr. David Hemenway is an economist and director of the Harvard Injury Control Research Center and the Harvard Youth Violence Prevention Center.*

Almost fifty people a day kill themselves with guns in the United States. These numbers increased 75 percent between 1965 and 1985 and have stayed reasonably constant since then. Since 1965, more than half a million Americans have committed suicide with a firearm, nearly ten times as many as have died from gun-related accidents.

In the United States, more people kill themselves with guns than by all other methods combined. Males are at high risk for suicide and for gun suicide in particular. Guns accounted for 61 percent of male suicides in 2000 but only 37 percent of female suicides. Still, guns are also the single most common means by which women kill themselves.

Among methods of suicide, firearms are typically the most lethal. For example, a study in Canada found that 92 percent of gun attempts result in death, compared to 78 percent of attempts using carbon monoxide or hanging, 67 percent of drowning attempts, and 23 percent of intentional drug overdoses. A study from Dallas found that of those attempting suicide with a gun, 76 percent died, while only 4 percent of those who attempted suicide by other means died. An eight-state study found that 82 percent of firearm suicide attempts resulted in death, compared to 61 percent for hanging/suffocation, 34 percent for jumping, 1.5 percent for drug poisoning, and 1.2 percent for cutting/piercing. A Chicago study

David Hemenway, "Gun-Related Injury and Death: Suicides," *Private Guns Public Health.* Ann Arbor: University of Michigan Press, 2004. Copyright © 2004 by David Hemenway. All rights reserved. Reproduced by permission.

found that more than 95 percent of attempted firearm suicides resulted in death. A recent study of northeast states examined suicidal acts serious enough to result in hospitalization or death. Over 90 percent of suicidal acts with a gun resulted in death, compared to 2 percent of drug overdoses and 3 percent of attempts by cutting or piercing. Drugs and cutting or piercing accounted for 94 percent of all nonfatal suicidal hospitalizations.

Suicide Variables

Among industrialized nations, the overall suicide rate in the United States falls roughly in the middle. However, our suicide rate for children five to fourteen years of age is twice the average of that in other developed countries because of our firearms-related suicide rate, which is ten times that of the average of the other nations. For fifteen- to twenty-four-year-olds, our firearm suicide rate is second only to Finland, but our overall suicide rate for this age group is only slightly above the average of other developed nations.

Many suicides appear to be impulsive acts.

Although the risk of suicide increases for the elderly, in comparison to most life-threatening diseases, suicide disproportionately affects younger people. Suicide accounts for 12 percent of all deaths among five- to twenty-four-year-olds, the third-leading cause of death behind only motor vehicle crashes (28 percent) and homicides (21 percent). In terms of the number of people dying, suicide is a young adult/middle age problem. In 2000, 57 percent of all suicide deaths were to individuals 25–54 years old.

Women attempt suicide roughly three times as often as men, yet more than four times as many men die. The gun suicide rate in 2000 was almost 7 times higher for men than for women; the nongun suicide rate was 2.5 times higher. Suicide rates are higher for whites than for nonwhites: in 2000, whites had twice the suicide rate of African Americans.

In addition to age, gender, and race, many other variables—including marital status, income, unemployment, and cigarette consumption—are associated with suicide rates. The strongest individual risk factor for attempting suicide is a psychiatric or substance abuse disorder. Although more than 90 percent of suicides are associated with a mental or addictive disorder, the parameters of what constitutes such a disorder are so broad that it is estimated that perhaps 30 percent of the U.S. population, or eighty million people, has one. Not surprisingly, this makes identifying individuals likely to commit suicide difficult indeed. As noted in one report, "There is no single, readily identifiable, high-risk population that constitutes a sizeable portion of overall suicides and yet represents a small, easily targeted group."

The problem of identifying those likely to commit suicide is particularly difficult among teenagers. A study of students in Massachusetts high schools found that 26 percent reported that they had seriously considered suicide, 18 percent had made plans, 10 percent had attempted suicide in the previous twelve months, and almost 4 percent needed medical attention. Studies show that more than 75 percent of all U.S. suicides are not in psychiatric treatment at the time of their death, and half do not appear to have had any prior treatment.

Many suicides appear to be impulsive acts. Individuals who take their own lives often do so when confronting a severe but temporary crisis. In one small study of men who survived self-inflicted intentional gunshot wounds to the face, few attempted suicide again. In another study of nearly lethal suicide attempts, 24 percent of attempters reported spending less than five minutes between the decision to attempt suicide and the actual attempt. In yet another study of self-inflicted gunshot wounds that would have been fatal without emergency treatment, none of the thirty attempters had written a suicide note, and more than half reported having suicidal thoughts for less than twenty-four hours. In two years of follow-up, none of the thirty attempted suicide again. As the lead researcher put it, "Many patients in our sample admitted that while they had originally expected to die, they were glad to be alive, and would not repeat the self-destructive behavior, despite the continued presence of significant medical, psychological and social problems". . . .

Gun Availability and Suicide

There has long been agreement that increased firearm availability increases the firearm suicide rate. However, a point of debate was whether gun availability increases the overall rate of suicide or whether suicidal individuals merely substitute other lethal means if guns are not available. [Gary] Kleck claims that "general gun ownership levels . . . appear to have no net effect on total suicide rates". This conclusion is contrary to the available evidence.

Three recent review articles conclude that the evidence shows that gun availability is a risk factor for suicide. For example, in the past twenty years, ten individual-level studies (case-control and cohort studies) have examined the relationship between gun ownership and suicide in the United States, and all find that firearms in the home are associated with substantially and significantly higher rates of suicide. . . .

Individuals in homes with handguns, loaded guns, and unlocked guns all had higher risks of suicide than other individuals.

Five overlapping studies by one research team have focused on adolescent suicides. One study found that guns were in the homes of 72 percent of the suicide victims but only 37 percent of the controls. Cases and controls were matched on age, gender, and county of origin. Even after matching and statistically accounting for other risk factors—such as psychiatric diagnosis, suicide intent, or presence of a male in the home—guns were significantly more likely to be found in the homes of suicide victims. Another in this series of case-control studies found that for adolescents with no apparent psychiatric disorders, handguns and loaded guns in the home present a particularly large relative risk of suicide. This finding suggests that the danger of having a gun in the home applies to all adolescents and not just to adolescents with known psychiatric or substance abuse problems.

Two large case-control studies have included both adults and adolescents. One focused on suicides that occurred at home in two urban areas: Shelby County, Tennessee, a predominantly poor black community, and King County, Washington, a predominantly upper-middle-class white community. This study found that 65 percent of the victims had firearms in the home, compared to 41 percent of the controls. After matching for age, gender, race, and neighborhood and statistically controlling for six variables—education, living alone, consumption of alcohol, previous hospitalization due to drinking, current use of prescription medication for depression or mental illness, and use of illicit drugs—the presence of a gun in the home was associated with a fivefold increase in the risk of suicide. Restricting the analysis to those suicides without a history of mental illness or depression revealed that guns were even more strongly associated with suicide. Individuals in homes with handguns, loaded guns, and unlocked guns all had higher risks of suicide than other individuals. Having any gun in the home was a risk factor for suicide for women as well as men, for whites, and for all age groups, but especially for adolescents and young adults. The major limitations of the study were that it examined only suicides that occurred in the home and relied on self-reports of household gun ownership.

Another large case-control study eliminated these problems by analyzing whether the purchase of a handgun from a licensed dealer (using information compiled by the dealers) was associated with an increased risk of suicide, whether or not the suicide took place in the home. Results showed that individuals who committed suicide were more likely than controls to have a family history of handgun purchase (25 versus 15 percent). The most serious limitations of this study were its inability to account for psychological risk factors such as a history of psychiatric disorders, previous suicide attempts, or substance abuse. However, it did seem to show that the higher risk for gun purchasers could not be fully explained by victims buying guns to commit suicide. While the relative risk for suicide was greatest within the first year after purchase, it remained elevated even after five years; the median interval between the first handgun purchase and any suicide with a gun was eleven years. The risk for suicide was higher for individuals with a family handgun purchase even if a family member other than the victim had purchased the gun. In other words, it appears that the association between guns in the home and suicide did not result from some individuals obtaining guns to commit suicide.

A recent case-control study found that among middle-aged and elderly adults, those with a gun in the home had higher rates of suicide. Presence of a firearm in the home was associated with an increased risk for suicide even after controlling for psychiatric illness. Among subjects who kept guns in the home, storing the weapon loaded and unlocked were independent predictors of suicide. Only 10 percent of firearm suicides had recently purchased the firearm. The results suggest that poor gun storage may increase the likelihood of suicide.

A national case-control study of U.S. adults for 1993/94, created by pooling two national surveys, found that a gun in the home was associated with a tripling of the likelihood of suicide; a handgun in the home posed a higher risk than a long gun. Fifty-three percent of case households had a handgun in the home compared to 20 percent of controls. The study controlled for age, gender, race, income, marital status, education, living alone, region, and population size. An analysis using similar data reached similar conclusions. A limitation of these large national studies was that data on gun presence was missing for 30 percent of case subjects.

Overall, the evidence summarized here on the gun-suicide connection within the United States is quite compelling—firearm availability appears to increase the rate of suicide.

Finally, a longitudinal cohort study found that during the first week after a handgun purchase, the rate of suicide was fifty-seven times higher than the age-adjusted rate for the general population. That finding suggests that individuals sometimes purchase guns with the immediate intention of killing themselves, but the study also found that the higher risk for suicide persisted for at least six years. Again the indication is that the gun-suicide connection does not result from depressed individuals purposely buying guns as a means to commit suicide. . . .

Relationship Between Suicide and Gun Control

A variety of studies have examined the relationship between the strictness of gun control laws and suicide rates. Many cross-sectional studies find that strict state gun control laws are significantly associated with lower levels of suicide. Time-series studies in the United States and Canada also find a significant reduction in suicide rates after the enactment of stringent gun control laws.

Overall, the evidence summarized here on the gun-suicide connection within the United States is quite compelling—firearm availability appears to increase the rate of suicide. Perhaps the best evidence concerning the connection between gun availability and suicide comes from the case-control studies. The results are persuasive in part because these studies account for many other important factors associated with suicide. The recent cross-sectional evidence—within the United States—showing a strong association between guns and suicides across states and regions is also quite persuasive, again because many other explanatory variables are taken into account. The studies linking gun control laws and suicide are suggestive.

The American Association of Suicidology consensus statement on youth suicide concludes,

> There is a positive association between the accessibility and availability of firearms in the home and the risk of youth suicide; guns in the home, particularly loaded guns, are associated with increased risk for suicide by youth, both with and without identifiable mental health problems or suicidal risk factors.

Many strategies can and should be used to reduce suicide, including school-dropout prevention and role modeling, suicide awareness among health professionals, substance abuse treatment, and training high-risk individuals in depression management and anger control. Educational campaigns are needed to help remove the stigma surrounding mental illness and increase awareness that clinical depression can often be effectively treated with antidepressant medications and talk therapy.

But based on all available data, one of the best strategies for reducing suicide appears to be the removal of firearms from the home, particularly where there are adolescents or young adults. The evidence supporting the effectiveness of removing guns is probably stronger than that for almost any other single suicide-prevention policy. Removing guns will not eliminate all or probably even most suicides. Some determined individuals will find ways to get guns or will choose alternative lethal methods. But many others will choose less lethal methods or may not even try at all.

Social Stigma Surrounding Mental Illness Contributes to Suicides Among Black Professionals

Keisha Gaye Anderson

About the author: *Keisha Gaye Anderson is the associate director of media relations and publications at Lehman College, the City University of New York, located in Bronx, New York.*

In 1995, Rene Ruballo noticed a troubling change within him. This now retired New York City police officer and father of four started losing interest in everything he once felt passionate about, including his police work and spending time with his family. At times he would ditch work and sleep all day. Other times, he'd function on only an hour's sleep. He no longer felt he had anything to look forward to in his life.

As he grew more and more withdrawn, Ruballo's family realized something was very wrong. "My wife and children saw that I wasn't interested in the things we used to do," says 43-year-old Ruballo. "If there were family outings, I used to just tell my wife, 'You can take [the kids].' And I would just stay home." Ruballo's wife urged him to seek counseling. Eventually he did get professional help, and his suspicions about the cause of his feelings were finally confirmed: He had depression.

Blacks Are Undertreated for Depression

Most people use the word depression to describe feeling sad or blue, but it is much more than that. This serious medical illness affects some 18 million Americans and can have debilitating effects on those who suffer from it. Twice as many women suffer from depression as men, but men are less likely to admit they are depressed or seek help. Across racial and ethnic lines, poor and less educated individuals suffer from higher rates of depression. And although depression goes largely undiagnosed among all ethnic groups, the disparities in treatment are stark in the African American community.

There still is a stigma in the African American community that psychotropic medications are being used as a social control mechanism.

"Non-Hispanic blacks and Hispanics both have lower rates of treatment than non-Hispanic whites," says Ronald Kessler, professor of healthcare policy at Harvard Medical School. "When they get treatment, furthermore, it is less likely to be in the specialty mental health sector and more likely to be treatment from a primary care physician or social worker or minister. This is a double disadvantage—lower overall treatment and presumably lower quality of treatment once in treatment." Social stigmas surrounding mental health in the African American community, as well as limited access to health plans that provide direct mental healthcare, contribute to undertreatment. Public health institutions are more likely to offer poor clients medication than psychotherapy.

"There still is a stigma in the African American community that psychotropic medications are being used as a social control mechanism," says Kessler. But depression, left untreated, can completely halt one's ability to function day to day and, at its worst, may even lead to suicide. There were 30,622 suicides in the U.S. in 2001, 1,957 of which were committed by African Americans, according to the American Association of Suicidology. This breaks down to 5.4 African Americans suicides per day.

Depression in the Corporate World

Depression is not uncommon among African American professionals and executives. "It's very difficult for African Americans in corporate settings, where they know they are being looked at closely," says Dr. Annelle B. Primm, associate professor of psychiatry at Johns Hopkins University School of Medicine. "They never know if they're being responded to for who they are as a person or who they are as an African American." She says that while the predisposition for depression is genetic, depressive symptoms may present themselves during stressful life events.

Since African American professionals usually face higher levels of scrutiny and common concerns such as the glass ceiling, stress and depression are not uncommon. "In the corporate sector, you think that people have 'arrived,' but they are not immune from getting the illness of depression. And if it is untreated and overlooked, there is a risk that it could end up being a fatal illness," says Primm. She adds that black professionals often feel they have to hide their depression for fear of damaging their careers and to feel secure in their positions. "They may feel that they've worked so hard to get to this point. They may fear getting treatment because it may impair their upward mobility or ability to maintain their status. You don't want to give anyone a competitive edge."

The dangers of such behavior are great. According to Primm, it's not uncommon for executives to try to "work through the depression," overwork to the point of exhaustion, or begin abusing substances. "Because of the realities of racism and how we as African Americans are judged differently, the risks of admitting we are ill are very high."

Causes of Depression

Not much is understood about the exact cause of depression, but we do know that it involves certain neurotransmitters, like dopamine and serotonin. People who are depressed often do not show enough serotonin activity, for example, and this is where antidepressant SSRI (selective serotonin reuptake inhibitor) medications might help. They include brand names like Paxil, Prozac, and Zoloft. But there are a host of other medications doctors might provide to treat varying degrees of depression.

New research is also uncovering strong links between depression and other debilitating diseases, such as cancer, heart disease, and diabetes. In fact, people with diabetes have a two-fold chance of getting depressed, and people with depression are twice as likely to get diabetes. Depression and diabetes involve a common part of the brain. They also both involve the stress hormone cortisol, too much of which is damaging to brain cells.

Although depression is an equal opportunity disease, manifestation of symptoms can differ widely among ethnic groups. "It's very unusual for an African American man to come in and say he's 'sad,' because it's not appropriate culturally for a black man to present himself that way," says Primm.

Admitting depression is a cultural taboo among African Americans.

Often, African American men and women will display their depression as anger or irritability instead of sadness. Changes in eating habits and complaints of chronic pain that no physical evidence can substantiate may also be red-flag indicators of depression in African Americans.

The Culture of Depression

Large-scale studies have typically shown African Americans have a lower rate of depression than the majority population. "Non-Hispanic blacks and Hispanics both have a significantly lower lifetime risk of ever becoming clinically depressed than non-Hispanic whites, but they also have higher risks of chronicity once they become depressed," says Kessler. But Dr. William Lawson, chair of the department of psychiatry at Howard University, says there might be a different reason that African Americans appear to have a lower risk for depression.

"We have different idioms of distress," says Lawson. "It's not always easy to convince others of the importance of cultural competence training. We speak a common language and we live in the same geographical area [as whites], so it is assumed that [even though] we may look a little different, we're really just white people when you scratch away the skin. But there are some profound cultural differences that are persistent and important, that need to be looked at." For one thing, admitting depression is a cultural taboo among African Americans. Lawson says he has worked with black churches where people were more ready to accept people with HIV than those who were depressed. In addition, since most African Americans will seek help from their primary care physician when faced with symptoms of depression before seeing a mental health professional, they are more likely to be given medication and nothing else.

"If a patient comes in and sits down and you give them pills, they're not going to take them," says Lawson. "African Americans will often prefer psychotherapy over medication, and the research shows that psychotherapy is just as helpful." In fact, the combination of psychotherapy and medication has frequently been shown to be effective in treating major and chronic depression. Lawson notes that there is a strong need for African Americans to be included in more clinical trials to determine how medications might affect them specifically. He also says that African Americans should generally be prescribed lower doses of some antidepressant medications because they metabolize them differently and therefore have higher instances of side effects.

Falling Prey to Mental Illness

"With respect to African Americans, falling prey to mental illness places you in a vulnerable position, and we're already in a vulnerable position," says Boris Thomas, a psychotherapist and social worker based in Chicago. Thomas acknowledges that the situational differences African Americans experience in this country because of race can be significant stressors that may cause depression in some people. "There's a great deal of pressure to succeed in society, but there's also pressure on that person to manage issues of race. Being depressed can feel like it affirms some kind of weakness." But he urges people to get control of depression because ignoring the symptoms will not make them go away. They might even get worse. "Understanding that other people have similar problems, or 'universalizing' an ailment, can be a great help and reduce the sense of isolation," he says. "In this regard, group therapy can be very effective."

For Ruballo, the changes he experienced were not subtle, and people who are truly depressed will be able to identify the severity of what they are feeling. "I was very outgoing [before]. I was very happy. It was a big change from being an extrovert to an introvert," he says. "Sometimes the kids felt that they had done something [wrong]. It wasn't them."

Ruballo had the support of his family when it came to seeking professional help, but many people don't have that support and delay treatment. If seeing a therapist is intimidating, talk to your primary care physician or consider group counseling. Talking to friends and family, even your minister, can be comforting. But ultimately, if you are experiencing prolonged symptoms (for more than two weeks) such as sleep disturbance, appetite changes, irritability, lack of concentration, or suicidal thoughts, you may have depression, and you should seek professional treatment.

Suicide Can Be a Fad
Among Teenagers

Vanessa Grigoriadis

About the author: *Vanessa Grigoriadis is a contributing editor to* New York *and* Rolling Stone *magazines.*

On the seventh-floor hallway of a gracious dorm on lower Fifth Avenue, photos of Stephen Bohler, the second of four undergraduates to jump to their deaths this academic year, are pinned to doors. A vast collage of yearbook-style tributes hangs on a cinder-block wall—"you're my hero, because you brought your own Tabasco to college." In his old room, a mess of boxes hunker next to his bed, now occupied by another student: sneakers, a cocktail shaker, [Albert] Camus's *The Plague*, a figurine of a baby that doubles as a lighter, a bag of decaying peppermint incense he bought in Washington Square Park. "We're going to take all of Stephen's old stuff to the Salvation Army," says one of his two former roommates, Jimmy Lynch. "Eventually."

This was the day that Diana Chien, a transfer student from UCLA, appeared on the cover of the *New York Post* leaping from her boyfriend's 24-story building, and a day before that boyfriend shared his plans to marry her in a posthumous ceremony in the same pages. At NYU, administrators were angry—they had spent time and money convening panels of experts, overhauling their mental-health services, and adding counselors after Bohler and the other two students died last autumn, and the last thing they needed was the *Post* in the picture. They didn't want to become known as a suicide university, like MIT, which is involved in a high-profile lawsuit about its responsibility in a student's suicide, or Cornell, where the stories of student plunges into snowy gorges are more lore than fact. "The NYU administration has a problem," says Edwin Shneidman, a prominent suicidologist and professor emeritus at UCLA. "This kind of thing affects funding and reputation and so on."

Suicide Is Contagious

NYU has a problem not because of anything it did or didn't do, but because suicide can be contagious. On one chilly Friday morning, I visited Madelyn Gould, an epidemiologist at Columbia University, one of the country's largest suicide research centers. "Suicide contagion is real," she said. "Social behavior is contagious and influential. We wouldn't have a billion-dollar advertising market in this country if people didn't think you could influence someone else's behavior."

There is some evidence that those who die in clusters wouldn't have acted on their own.

Before a monthly departmental lunch—"pizza, not hemlock"—Gould walked me through the basics of studies on suicide contagion. Research has shown that those who are most at risk after a suicide within a particular community are not the initial victim's immediate circle of family and friends but those who did not know the deceased at all. The classic case is Marilyn Monroe's suicide—for the month after her August 1962 death, researchers found that 197 more suicides than usual occurred nationwide, an increase of 12 percent. (Remarkably, few copycat suicides were documented after Kurt Cobain's death, a dearth researchers have attributed to Courtney Love's emotional denunciation of his act—"I want you all to say 'asshole' really loud." No one wanted to be an asshole.)

Those who are most susceptible to this contagion are teenagers (think of *The Virgin Suicides*, or *Heathers*). "Suicide clusters," as the phenomenon is called, occur with few exceptions among those 15 to 24 years of age. "As in many things, adolescents are more imitative in suicide," says David Phillips, a sociologist at the University of California at San Diego. "Look at hairstyles, slang, clothing styles, and popular music—adolescents are much more preoccupied with copying than older people. Their identity is not yet formed, so they're more concerned with looking like others."

Suicide as Fad

There are likely other factors in play—late adolescence is often the age at which serious psychological disorders, like bipolarity and schizophrenia, first manifest, and psychiatrists note that a suicide in the midst is a trigger mainly to those already thinking about suicide. But there is some evidence that those who die in clusters wouldn't have acted on their own. Phillips calls this the Werther Effect, named for the spurned lover in Goethe's *The Sorrows of Young Werther*—Werther, in a blue waistcoat and yellow vest, sits down one night, writes the object of his desire a last letter, and shoots himself above his right eye. Soon after the book's publication in 1774, young men dressed as Werther began to shoot themselves at desks with open books in front of them, and the novel was subsequently banned across Italy, Germany, and Denmark.

In fact, the idea of suicide as fad is the one that fits most closely the death of Stephen Bohler. He was a popular kid—a juggler, a diver, a poet, always dashing uptown to play soccer in Central Park. He was a liberal, a vegetarian, a conscientious objector. He wanted to write a book called *My Life As a Non-Fighter*, and talked about it in a school essay: "I have not begun the book, but I have not really lived my life," he wrote.

Bohler was thoughtful, but no one describes him as unhappy. The day that he died, he had taken psilocybin mushrooms; hallucinations are thought to have played a part in his death (in a controversial decision, the medical examiner's office deemed his leap an accident). Friends say he smoked a lot of pot, and projected a stoner image—in touch with his emotions, but above it all. These days, his family goes back to a prose poem he wrote, titled "The Subjective Pronoun Me": "Nervous kept yelling at Curious to stop going so far out into the ocean. Baffled watched Inspired build a beautiful sandcastle. Selfish was busy stuffing sand into his pockets. Crafty seemed to be making some kind of submarine out of seashells . . . All this I watched (Attentive made me) quietly under a palm tree . . . My emotions returned to me one by one as I slept in the warm sun. Confused wanted to be last, but he was finally coaxed in before Calm returned."

There is no evidence that any of the four students to die at NYU were acquainted with each other. But when John Skolnik, the first jumper, leaped from the tenth-floor atrium balcony of the university's main library—not quite the Golden Gate Bridge, but possessed of a vertiginous spookiness all its own—Bohler heard about it. He wasn't obsessed with it, and he didn't talk about it a lot, but he knew. He even mentioned it to his mother, Carolyn Bohler, a Methodist minister. And Skolnik, for his part, knew the legend about the library, the one passed from senior to freshman, the one each student, shivering and smoking in front of the library the other day, could retell: The Escher-like mosaic on the ground floor was supposedly designed to appear as spikes from several stories above, the better to deter potential jumpers.

There is some logic behind suicide clusters. The first suicide might give permission to others to carry out the act themselves—much like the teenager's friend who smokes, or the driver in front of you who speeds. It may also look like the deceased has gotten some sort of reward—attention, pity, maybe higher social status than when he was alive. Beyond this, there are precipitating factors that no one will ever know about, except for the person who can't talk about them anymore. "I don't know if Stephen jumped because of the first boy, or because of the legends, or because he was hallucinating," says Carolyn Bohler. "But almost nothing happens because of one cause."

Unfortunately, there may sometimes seem to be only one solution. "Suicide is an advertisement for a way out of your problems," he says, "and as with any advertising, if it's repeated, it's more effective."

Suicide by Pesticides Is Common in Developing Countries

David Gunnell and Michael Eddleston

About the authors: *David Gunnell is a professor of epidemiology at the University of Bristol, United Kingdom. Dr. Michael Eddleston is an epidemiologist at the Centre for Tropical Medicine, University of Oxford, United Kingdom.*

Deliberate self-poisoning has become an increasingly common response to emotional distress in young adults, and it is now one of the most frequent reasons for emergency hospital admission. In industrialized countries, the drugs that people commonly take in overdose—analgesics, tranquillisers, antidepressants—are relatively non-toxic. The estimated case fatality for overdose in England, for example, is around 0.5%. Most individuals who self-harm do not intend to die. Studies carried out in industrialized countries have found that only 2% go on to commit suicide in the subsequent 12 months.

In developing countries the situation is quite different. The substances most commonly used for self-poisoning are agricultural pesticides. Overall case fatality ranges from 10% to 20%. For this reason, deaths from pesticide poisoning make a major contribution to patterns of suicide in developing nations, particularly in rural areas. In rural China, for example, pesticides account for over 60% of suicides. Similarly high proportions of suicides are due to pesticides in rural areas of Sri Lanka (71%), Trinidad (68%), and Malaysia (>90%). There is, however, no evidence that levels of suicidal intent associated with pesticide ingestion in these countries are any higher

David Gunnell and Michael Eddleston, "Suicide by Intentional Ingestion of Pesticides: A Continuing Tragedy in Developing Countries," *International Journal of Epidemiology*, vol. 32, 2003. © International Epidemiological Association 2003. All rights reserved. Republished with permission of Oxford University Press, conveyed through Copyright Clearance Center, Inc.

than those associated with drug overdose in industrialized countries, where the drugs taken in overdose are less toxic.

Pesticide Poisoning in Developing Countries

In countries where the use of pesticides for self-harm is commonplace conventional epidemiological features of suicide appear to be distorted. In industrialized nations, suicide rates are two to three times higher in men than women, and its incidence tends to increase with age, although in some countries recent rises in young male suicides have distorted this pattern. The incidence of non-fatal self-harm in industrialized countries is 20+ times higher than that of suicide; in contrast to suicide, self-harm rates peak in 15–24 year olds and are generally highest in women.

A possible explanation for these differences in the age- and sex-patterning of fatal and non-fatal self-harm is that young people, particularly females, are more likely to engage in impulsive acts of self-harm—as indicated by the comparatively lower levels of suicidal intent in young people. Because these acts are unplanned, the methods used are those that are readily available at the time of acute distress—prescribed and non-prescribed medicines—and these are relatively non-toxic. If more lethal methods of self-harm, such as pesticides, were favoured and readily accessible in industrialized nations the epidemiology of suicide in these countries might be quite different. Thus the widespread availability of pesticides may contribute to the difference in the age- and sex-patterning of suicide in China, Sri Lanka, India, and several other developing countries compared with that commonly seen in industrialized nations. In these developing countries some of the highest rates are seen in young adults and the ratio of male:female suicide approaches or exceeds unity at this age.

In China, whilst suicide rates do tend to increase with age, there is a notable peak in rates amongst males and females aged 20–24; recent data show that this peak is more prominent in rural localities. In rural India rates of suicide in 15–24 year old females are higher than rates in males of the same age and most other female age groups. Similar patterns are seen in Sri Lanka. In both China and Sri Lanka pesticides are the most frequently used method of suicide, likewise in India self-poisoning is the commonest method and pesticides are the most frequently used agents. It is of note that the age- and sex-patterns of self-poisoning in Sri Lanka in the younger age groups are similar to those in industrialized countries, although in contrast, the case fatality in Sri Lanka is much higher.

There is general consensus that the ease of availability of particularly lethal means of self-harm may influence patterns of suicide.

Part of the distinct age- and gender-patterns of suicide deaths in the developing world may therefore reflect a mixture of deaths with high suicidal intent (predominantly in the elderly) and an excess of deaths with low suicidal intent amongst the young where the method chosen for impulsive acts of self-harm (pesticide ingestion) is highly lethal. A possibility strikingly born out in Western Samoa in the 1980s, where two-thirds of all suicides were a result of pesticide ingestion and the age- and sex-patterning of suicide and non-fatal self-harm were almost identical.

The Easy Availability of Pesticides

The common use of pesticides for self-harm in part reflects their ease of availability. Whilst their use in agriculture is widespread in industrialized countries, large-scale farming is practised by a small number of landowners, thus reducing the number of people with direct access to pesticides. In contrast, most people living in rural regions of developing countries are involved in agriculture and farm small areas of land. Subsistence farmers keep their own supply of pesticides, commonly within, or close to, the household. A recent study in China found that 65% of pesticide suicides used chemicals stored in the home.

There is general consensus that the ease of availability of particularly lethal means of self-harm may influence patterns of suicide. Suicidal impulses are often short lived and if time can be 'bought' allowing such impulses to pass—by making the means of suicide less readily available—a proportion of suicides will be prevented. The best documented evidence of this was the effect of the detoxification of the domestic gas supply in Britain in the 1960s—this was thought to have contributed to the prevention of an estimated 6,700 suicides. Similarly, temporal and geographical variations in the availability of other commonly used methods have influenced patterns of suicide in Australia (barbiturates), USA (firearms), and Britain (catalytic converters for car exhaust fumes).

This evidence has prompted the inclusion of policies aimed at reducing access to, or the lethality of, commonly used methods within national and international suicide prevention strategies. In Britain attention has focused on restricting the availability of paracetamol (acetaminophen) and in the USA there are similar concerns about the ease of availability of firearms.

There are around 300 000 pesticide suicides each year in [China and Southeast Asia] alone.

The number of deaths caused by pesticides make Western concerns about these two methods of suicide appear somewhat trivial. For example, in Britain where paracetamol suicide is comparatively common, there are only around 200 paracetamol suicides per year (<4% of all suicides). If a similar proportion of suicides were due to paracetamol worldwide (an overestimate) then using the [World Health Organization]

WHO's current estimate of 849,000 suicides worldwide each year a maximum of 34,000 of these might be attributable to paracetamol.

In contrast, the WHO estimated in 1990 that there are around 3 million hospital admissions for pesticide poisoning each year, 2 million of which are as a result of deliberate ingestion, and these result in around 220,000 deaths. The size of the problem is probably larger now—there have, for example, been well-recognized increases in pesticide poisonings in South Asia.

The best evidence for estimating the global burden of suicide deaths from pesticide ingestion comes from China and South East Asia. In 2001 there were an estimated 517,000 suicides in developing countries in these regions and research evidence (see above) suggests pesticide ingestion accounts for over 60% of these suicides. We therefore estimate there are around 300,000 pesticide suicides each year in these regions alone. As pesticide suicides from other developing nations in Africa and South America are not included in this figure the global toll is likely to be higher. . . .

Ways to Reduce Pesticide Poisoning

The first broad approach is to restrict the availability of pesticides either directly, for example through restricting the import and use of pesticides, or indirectly through ensuring supplies are kept in a secure facility in each geographical locality. Restricting availability could be achieved by either direct control of particular pesticides (banning, requiring licences for use or prescriptions) or through the promotion of practices that minimize their use. Such health protection approaches appear to have led to a reduction in serious paracetamol poisonings in England and a decline in barbiturate suicides in Australia. The WHO has encouraged countries to restrict the availability of more lethal pesticides and countries such as Sri Lanka have followed this approach. In Jordan, a steady rise in fatal pesticide poisonings was reversed by increased awareness of the problem, decreased imports of some toxic pesticides, and bans on the imports of others. Similar effects have been observed in Western Samoa after reduced use of paraquat and a campaign to raise awareness of suicide; however, here fluctuations in imports were driven by the nation's financial problems rather than a concern with suicide.

The lethality of pesticide poisoning is for the most part due to the difficulty of treatment and their greater toxicity compared with substances taken in overdose in industrialized countries.

The second approach is to improve public education regarding the dangers of pesticide poisoning and the safekeeping of pesticides—through media campaigns and clear labelling of product containers. The effects are difficult to predict and there is a suggestion that enhanced knowledge concerning the toxicity of pesticides resulted in an increase in their use for self-harm in some settings. Furthermore, it is widely recognized that media portrayal of acts of self-harm can lead to increases in 'copy-cat' suicides.

The third general approach is to encourage manufacturers to improve the safety of their products. This may be achieved by diluting the concentrations of liquid pesticides, incorporating emetics or agents to make them unpleasant to taste or, more fundamentally, to produce pesticides which are non-toxic to humans. Company responsibility for the safe use of pesticides should extend for the entire life cycle of their use.

Lastly, if the occurrence and lethality of pesticide ingestions cannot be prevented then improved medical management is crucial. The lethality of pesticide poisoning is for the most part due to the difficulty of treatment and their greater toxicity compared with substances taken in overdose in industrialized countries. Antidotes to pesticides are not completely effective. In rural areas, where the majority of cases occur, health care is often distant and of poor 'quality'. In the UK, where paracetamol is the most common poison used for self-harm, a similar situation could be envisaged if all the antidotes became unavailable—the medical wards might once again become filled with paracetamol-poisoned patients with either anticipated or florid liver failure.

Reasons for the Lack of Global Response

The problem of death from pesticide self-poisoning is neither new nor unique to a few countries, so reasons for the lack of a global response need to be understood if this continuing tragedy is to be reversed.

Five main factors appear to contribute. First, the pattern of agriculture practised in developing countries—where most people living in rural areas cultivate small areas of land—is quite different from that in industrialized nations where a small number of farmers cultivate large tracts of land. In industrialized countries access to pesticides is therefore largely restricted to the few individuals engaged in farming. In developing nations pesticides are available within most peoples' place of residence. Interventions to limit access in such settings are complex and need to involve most rural adults, rather than a select few.

Second, the sale of pesticides is a multi-billion dollar business. In all, 1.5 million tons of pesticides are sold annually and sales are worth an estimated US$30 billion. Tensions commonly exist between commercial interests and population health, furthermore industry has not always acknowledged the impact of the easy availability of lethal suicide methods on patterns of suicide. In describing Western Samoa's preventive considerations following the epidemic rise in pesticide suicides in that country [JR] Bowles noted:

> There was at that time a contentious debate about actually banning paraquat [(the pesticide)] entirely. We knew how-

ever that there were powerful and influential people who had a vested interest in continuing the importation and we did not want to be aligned with a lobby group likely to fail.

Third, the issue of pesticide self-poisoning has never been taken up as a campaign issue by any of the international organizations. The WHO is the pre-eminent public health organization and its Department of Mental Health and Substance Dependence (MNH) is responsible for suicide prevention. It has managed to successfully draw mental health up the worldwide political agenda over the last 10 years. It has also emphasized the global health importance of suicide, organizing workshops across the world to discuss strategies for reducing self-harm, but it has not taken up pesticides as a central issue. Recent WHO publications with major input from the MNH have put greater emphasis on psychiatric and social models of self-harm aetiology. While pesticide self-poisoning was mentioned in both reports, it received much less attention than its importance warrants.

Pesticide self-poisoning is ideologically and politically inconvenient.

The International Programme on Chemical Safety (IPCS) is the major WHO programme dealing with pesticides. It was set up in 1980 by the United Nations Environment Programme, the International Labour Organization, and the WHO, to establish the scientific basis for safe use of chemicals and to strengthen national capabilities for chemical safety. Current IPCS activities aim to increase knowledge of the epidemiology of pesticide poisoning and to encourage the setting up of poisoning information centres. The IPCS has not, however, actively taken up the issue of intentional pesticide self-poisoning, concentrating instead on occupational and environmental poisoning. This is unfortunate since its own studies have indicated the great importance of self-poisoning in the

Asia Pacific region. The interests of its parent organizations may be the reason for this lack of advocacy for the problem of intentional poisoning.

Fourth, the self-inflicted nature of suicide, together with the fact there are fewer suicide deaths than deaths from other global health problems such as human immunodeficiency virus (HIV)/AIDS, tuberculosis, and malaria, may have led to policy makers giving it lower priority than the number of premature deaths warrant.

Fifth, pesticide self-poisoning is ideologically and politically inconvenient. Pesticide use has adverse effects on the environment and human health. This has become a major global political issue. Many of the adverse effects of pesticides are considered to result from their overuse and poor treatment of workers and communities due to globalization—in which pesticide corporations are major participants. The issue has been taken up by numerous national and international non-governmental organizations (NGO), in continual 'battle' with the pesticide companies. In this battle, the fact that the vast majority of severe and fatal pesticide cases are self-inflicted may be inconvenient to the environmentalists. If the pesticide industry can argue that they should not be held responsible for people who drink pesticides, then this may be seen as undermining the environmentalists' case. People therefore want to avoid the issue of self-poisoning and deal with issues where the pesticide industry, and globalization in general, can be held responsible.

This need not be true. An overall assessment of public health, environmental and agricultural factors should determine regulatory actions, not simply their political appropriateness. Pesticide self-harm is just as important as occupational poisoning for regulatory issues and, in some countries, regulatory authorities have been very effective in banning the pesticides that have been problems only for self-harm.

The Need for Additional Research

Pesticide self-poisoning is a major contributor to population patterns of morbidity and mortality in developing nations. The use of pesticides for self-poisoning may distort conventional epidemiological features of suicide in these countries and contribute to their excess premature mortality. We estimate there are around 300 000 self-inflicted pesticide deaths worldwide each year. Research dating back over 30 years has documented the size of this problem and yet contemporary research bears witness to its continuing impact.

Research to identify the most acceptable means of restricting the availability of pesticides within rural communities is urgently required together with randomized controlled trials to determine the best means of treatment and cost-effectiveness of possible interventions. Some of this research is now underway. Preventive measures must take account of the local needs and context and should be rigorously evaluated.

Thus far there has been no global leadership to respond to the problem. Engagement of national governments and leadership of the WHO, in particular the MNH and IPCS sections, on the issue is essential. Commitment from industry and the need for them to acknowledge their responsibility for some of these deaths is vital, as is the need to ensure they understand the scale, importance, and preventability of the problem. Reducing the number of pesticide deaths by 50% could rapidly reduce the number of suicides worldwide by 150 000. This is quite possible.

Many Women Suicide Bombers Are Sexual Abuse Victims

Mia Bloom

About the author: *Mia Bloom is a professor in the School of International and Public Affairs at the University of Georgia in Athens. She is also a term member of the Council on Foreign Relations.*

"Y̶ou've come a long way, baby!" Virginia Slims cigarette ads used to read. After years of struggle, the women's movement in the 1970s brought men and women in the first world to a level of relative parity in most areas of employment, status, and opportunities. However, in the rest of the world, the position of women remains seriously disadvantaged compared to that of men. According to a well cited [United Nations Development Programme] [(UNDP)] report, women in Africa and the Middle East suffer most from inequality. In one area, however, women in the developing world seem to be making their mark in achieving parity with men—in perpetrating suicide terrorism. The common stereotype is exploited by terrorists in order to magnify their cause is that women are gentle, submissive and nonviolent. On the one hand, despite the prejudices describing women as good wives and mothers, they are still capable of murder by engaging in suicide terror.

Historically, women have been involved in conflict in supporting roles. Most often, women's primary contribution has been to perpetuate the conflict by giving birth to many fighters and raising them in a revolutionary environment.

Society, through its body of rules and its numerous institutions, has conventionally dictated [women's] roles within the boundaries of militancy. Assisting in subordinate roles is welcomed and encouraged . . . fighting in the war is not. Yet women have demanded to be integrated in all aspects of war including frontline fighting.

What is incredibly compelling about delving into how and why women become suicide bombers is that so many of these women have been raped or sexually abused in the previous conflict.

According to many International Relations theories, women are more likely to choose peaceful mechanisms for conflict resolution than men—suggesting that women are inherently more peaceful in their attitudes toward international conflict and are more disposed toward moderation, compromise, and tolerance. What previously seemed highly unlikely because of the existing notions of women as *victims* of war rather than as perpetrators, women are now taking a leading role in conflicts by becoming suicide bombers—using their bodies as human detonators for the explosive material strapped around their waists. To complicate the notions of femininity and motherhood, the Improvised Explosive Device (IED) is often disguised under the woman's clothing to make her appear as if she is pregnant and thus beyond suspicion or reproach. The advent of women suicide bombers has transformed the revolutionary womb into an exploding one. Approximately 17 groups have started using the tactical innovation of suicide bombing, women have been operatives in more than half of them in the Middle East, in Sri Lanka, in Turkey, in Chechnya, and in Colombia.

Why? Motives vary: revenge for a personal loss, the desire to redeem the family name, to escape a life of sheltered monotony and achieve fame, and to level the patriarchal societies in which they live. What is incredibly compelling about delving into how and why women become suicide bombers is that so many of these women have been raped or sexually abused in the previous conflict either by the representatives of the state or by the insurgents themselves. Targeting women through rape in war has many unintended consequences which I explore elsewhere. . . .

Female Suicide Bomber Motivations

When men conduct suicide missions, they are motivated by religious or nationalist fanaticism, whereas women appear more often motivated by very personal reasons. In Chechnya [Russia], the female operatives called "Black Widows"—operatives who have lost a loved one—are mobilized by their personal tragedy.

> Zarema Mazhikhoyeva, a widow from Ingushetia, was arrested as she walked along 1st Tverskaya Yamskaya Ulitsa on July 10, 2003, carrying a homemade bomb. In an interview published in *Izvestia*, Mazhikhoyeva agreed to be recruited by Chechen rebels as a suicide bomber, in exchange for $1,000 in compensation to her relatives to repay for jewelry she had stolen from them. . . . When the rebels sent her to Moscow to carry out her mission, she changed her mind and got herself arrested by police.

Mazhikhoyeva was the first bomber to be captured alive. When the court convicted her and gave her the maximum sentence of twenty years regardless of the fact that she had voluntarily opted not to explode her cargo, Zarema shouted, "Now I know why everyone hates the Russians!"—adding that she would return and "blow you all up."

Women are not new to insurgent or terrorist activities.

Palestinian women have likewise suffered personal losses and some feel that becoming a martyr is their sole expression of outrage. Palestinian women are also motivated by the desire to recover their family honor. [Sri Lankan] Tamil women allegedly raped by the Sinhalese [the main ethnic group in Sri Lanka] security services and military at check points join the Tamil Tigers [rebels], joining the "birds of paradise" unit of Black Tigresses, while Kurdish women allegedly raped in Turkey by the military joined the [Kurdistan Workers Party] (PKK). Additionally, the insurgent organizations may provide a potential avenue for advancement beyond what their traditional societies offer.

> There is a difference between men and women suicide attackers: women consider combat as a way to escape the predestined life that is expected of them. When women become human bombs, their intent is to make a statement not only in the name of a country, a religion, a leader, but also in the name of their gender.

Women Terrorist Activities

Women are not new to insurgent or terrorist activities. Revolutionary women in radical secular organizations have engaged in anti-colonial and revolutionary struggles in the Third World and elsewhere. Female terrorists have come from all parts of the globe; Italy's Red Brigades, Germany's Baader-Meinhof faction, The Black Panthers, the Weathermen, and the Japanese Red Army—occasionally even as leaders in their own right. Women have played vital support roles in the Algerian Revolution (1958–1962), the Revolution in Iran (1979), in the War in Lebanon (1982), the First Palestinian Intifada (1987–1991) and the current Al Aqsa Intifada (since 2000). Women have supported the revolution, constructed the identities and ideologies of children, and funneled arms and ammunition to the men. In a few instances, women have been on the front lines of combat demonstrating that their revolutionary and military zeal is no less than that of the men. Even Al Qaeda has used women but only for fulfilling tasks in the rear.

105

Palestinian women have been implicated in terrorism for more than thirty years. Dalai Maghribi was involved in one of the worst terrorist incidents in Israel's history when more than thirty passengers were massacred in a bus hijacking in March 1978. In 1970, Leila Khaled, was caught after attempting to hijack an El Al flight to London. In her book, she explains a woman's rationale. For Khaled, violence was a way of leveling the patriarchal society through revolutionary zeal— the women would demonstrate that their commitment was no less than those of their brothers, sons, or husbands. Strategically, women were able to gain access to areas where men had greater difficulty because the other side assumed that the women were second class citizens in their own society—dumb, illiterate perhaps, and incapable of planning an operation. According to Khaled in an interview with the *Corriere Della Sera*, "We [Palestinians] are under attack . . . [and] women are ready to sacrifice themselves for the national struggle for the respect of just rights." Men gained prestige and status from sustained militancy, "women gain status if they go beyond what is expected and achieve martyrdom or are wounded, carry out incredibly heroic acts, or abide by high moral standards."

According to some authors, women have been radicalized because the Israeli Defense Forces (IDF) and the security apparatus, the Shin Bet, have deliberately targeted them in specific ways as to exploit the patriarchal divisions within their society.

Suha describes a recent incident—one among many, she says—when she was traveling between the West Bank cities of Nablus and Ramallah. She says an Israeli soldier forced her and a man to sit in the dirt at a checkpoint for an hour. He gave them no reason for the delay. "He started by verbally abusing me. The way he was looking at my ID card was humiliating, not to mention the [sexual] passes (that Israeli soldiers) make at us women," she says. "Life is worth nothing when [we] are being humiliated on a daily basis."

In Turkey and Sri Lanka, women's militant activism has a different history—women have participated fully in the early stages of the political resistance at all levels. Women in Sri Lanka fight on the front lines and have their own military units in the [Liberation Tigers of Tamil Eelam] LTTE. Palestinian women's participation as suicide bombers or those in Chechnya emerged recently, and against all expectations. In the past, only secular nationalist organizations like the LTTE, Al-Aqsa Martyr's Brigades, or the PKK permitted women to be suicide bombers. Islamic religious organizations, like Hamas, initially refused to permit women to become martyrs and turned at least one woman away (Darine Abu Aisha, who joined one of the secular groups and committed the act on their behalf). Although a patriarchal structure dominates all these societies, the degree to which women participate actively or in support roles varies from place to place and appears to be evolving. Nevertheless, women's roles on the front lines of conflict remained the exception rather than rule. . . .

In Sri Lanka or in Turkey, female members of the terrorist organizations were encouraged to participate in suicide bombing and coerced by peer pressure.

Women Suicide Bombers and Gender

When analyzing female suicide bombings, specifying the terrorist organization and the larger society from which the women come become important factors in the analysis. Boaz Ganor of the International Institute for Counter-Terrorism says, "if you analyze the motivations of women who commit such attacks, it's the same as the men: they believe they are committed, patriotic, and this is combined with a religious duty. Many were not trained or prepared psychologically for the suicide attack."

However, the reasons for women's participation vary greatly from country to country. Past experience shows that there is generally no single overriding motivation, but rather a number of overlapping motivations working in concert.

> These motivations interact with the potential attacker's emotional predispositions, creating an explosive mixture that needs only some traumatic event to release all its hidden destructive energy. A skillful terrorist operative can easily identify a candidate in this emotional state, and coolly manipulate her into becoming a weapon for his organization.

Similarities exist between the cases. In Sri Lanka or in Turkey, female members of the terrorist organizations were encouraged to participate in suicide bombing and coerced by peer pressure. Both the Tamils and the Kurds share common features such as traditional societies where women's roles are determined and static. The LTTE and the PKK offered women the opportunity that no other arrangement in society could ever offer them, a degree of equality. Both groups were commanded by charismatic, unchallenged leaders, who trained women to kill and die for the cause. Women were also eager to prove their devotion to the group, or were dictated to do so, as has been pointed out earlier concerning Sri Lanka.

According to several of the preliminary studies that have been done on Palestinian female bombers, they represent a new model of suicide attackers. Seven women who, because of their gender, do not—or at least did not—fit the established profile of a Palestinian suicide bomber: one a seamstress, one an ambulance worker, two in college, one in high school, one a law school graduate, and one mother of two who left families stricken and shocked. Some analysts have suggested that these women were misfits or outcasts in their society. An article on the Israeli government website states:

> Any hint of impropriety, no matter how minor, can have serious consequences for the woman involved, even prompt-

ing male family members to murder her in a so-called "honor" killing. Such personal motives have been well exploited by the terrorist organizations when they approach women in order to recruit them for suicide attacks. Recent intelligence information, gathered by Israeli liaison and coordination officials, have identified a clear effort ... to recruit as suicide terrorists those young women who find themselves in acute emotional distress due to social stigmatization.

Women Hope to Reclaim Honor

Barbara Victor corroborates this hypothesis when she links the first four female Palestinian suicide bombers as having been placed in positions where the act of martyrdom was their sole chance to reclaim the family honor that had been lost by their own actions or the actions of other family members. Allegations abound that the first female Hamas suicide bomber, Reem Riashi, was coerced by both her husband and lover—as a way of saving face after an extramarital affair. Thus at some level, all the women were motivated by highly charged emotional and personal reasons. The suicide bombers who brought down Russian jets in August 2004 were two women who were unable to have children, a source of stigma in Chechen society. Finally, there is evidence that the women who were previously raped and ordinarily killed themselves (to avoid bringing shame on the family) are now being funneled into the Black Widows. During the first Chechen War there was a significant rise in women who committed suicide—including many who were expecting. The numbers of women who committed suicide dropped during the second Chechen War. According to Valerie Zawilski, the same women who committed suicide before were being funneled into the insurgent organizations.

The selection of women for suicide operations and the methods used to persuade them are similar in some respects to those employed for men, across a range of countries and cultures and by both secular and religious organizations.

> Taking advantage of candidates' innocence, enthusiasm, loss of focus and often personal distress and thirst for revenge, "persuaders" subject women as well as men to intense indoctrination and manipulation. They offer the would-be bombers a sense of direction, as well as seemingly magical solutions to their problems, overlaid with national or religious symbolism, and promises of concrete [financial] rewards for them and their families, in the next world if necessary.

However, there are allegations that women are subjected to special treatment by the recruiters such that women are abused in some fashion deliberately to coerce them into becoming bombers. In addition to Israeli allegations that Palestinian women have been deliberately seduced by militants who used their violation of the honor code to convert them to bombers, in Sri Lanka there have been similar allegations that Tamil insurgent groups have used all means at their disposal to induce women to join the organizations.

In the fall of 2002 three young Tamil women presented themselves to an international aid organization claiming that they had been raped by persons who spoke to them in Sinhalese but discovered later on that their attackers were Tamils. Although the women did not report the attacks, they were approached within days by members of the LTTE and coerced into becoming Black Tigresses—to recover the family honor of having had sex with Sinhalese men. Such allegations are shocking since the LTTE traditionally has never abused women nor has advocated or permitted the use of rape against enemy women. Several young women have been kidnapped by the LTTE and eventually escaped back to their villages. The Sri Lankan police established a set of parameters wherein women who were kidnapped had to report to the local police station and fill out a report detailing their experience. To make matters worse, by admitting LTTE membership, the police occasionally used this information as an excuse to rape the women and so they have faced a lose-lose scenario.

The common link between the cases, whether they reflect the facts or construct a fiction, is that women are more vulnerable in such patriarchal settings and occasionally susceptible to mobilization against their will.

Antidepressants Can Result in Suicide

Angela Bischoff

About the author: *Angela Bischoff researches, writes, and publicly speaks about the dangers of antidepressant drugs. She is also Tooker Gomberg's surviving spouse.*

I lost my best friend. I'm a suicide survivor. My soul-mate of 17 years, Tooker Gomberg, suicided on March 3, 2004. My life was turned upside down—I lost my best friend and the world lost a warrior.

The pain around suicide is unfathomable, and indescribable, for those left behind, but especially for the person driven to take his/her own life. Unless you've been there, you just can't know this darkest torture of the soul. I saw Tooker's anguish, an anguish so deep and riveting that he saw no choice other than to end the suffering through death.

What could possibly drive him to such despair?

A Tragic Suicide

Tooker Gomberg, internationally renowned environmental, peace and justice activist, gave up the ghost at age 48. He was in an excellent relationship for 17 years; he had skills and friends; he was kind, humorous, courageous, a fighter, a leader, an environmental and social justice advocate; and he had fame and respect around the world.

His first depression hit in 2001–02 following the free trade agreement protest police clamp-down and horrific mass poisoning (tear gas, etc.) in Quebec City. Tooker was discouraged and exhausted, and his depression zapped the spark out of him for nine months. He tried many holistic alternatives to pharmaceutical drugs before turning to an [selective serotonin reuptake inhibitor (SSRI) antidepressant drug. Nothing seemed to help but, in time, he climbed out of his despair.

When his second depression hit a year later after moving to a new city and being unemployed, he sought help through counseling and pharmaceutical drugs, partly because he was desperate, but also because that was the only option the health care system would pay for. Psychiatrists are covered and the drugs they prescribe are covered, but doctors of Naturopathic medicine aren't, nor are Cognitive Behavioral Therapists, massage therapists or acupuncturists, etc.

Three weeks after Tooker died, the U.S. Food and Drug Administration (FDA) publicly associated antidepressant drugs with worsened depression and suicidal ideation.

Tooker's doctor prescribed Remeron, an antidepressant drug in a class of its own, but sometimes referred to as an [serotonin-norepinephrine reuptake inhibitor (SNRI). His anxiety and agitation went through the roof—clearly an adverse reaction—however his psychiatrist didn't perceive it as such, and encouraged him to stick with the program, increasing the dosage to the maximum. After just five weeks on the drug, Tooker's agitation sent him over the railing of the MacDonald Bridge in Halifax, Nova Scotia.

He wrote in his suicide note that he was anxious, felt like a zombie and couldn't think.

Suicide and Antidepressants

Three weeks after Tooker died, the U.S. Food and Drug Administration (FDA) publicly associated antidepressant drugs with worsened depression and suicidal ideation. I was dumbfounded and immediately immersed myself in this field, reading everything I could on what had been written to corroborate this bold assertion. It became obvious to me that Tooker was most definitely affected adversely by the drug he was on.

I'm no expert. I'm not a scientist. I'm a survivor who was motivated to peek behind the corporate curtain and study what the independent experts were saying about the connection between antidepressant drugs and suicide. And what I learned astounded me.

I read the writings of two experts: Dr. David Healy from England and Dr. Peter Breggin from the U.S., both distinguished physicians of high academic standing and international credibility. Much of what they published in their books came from years in the courts as medical experts, pouring over company data made available through court injunctions previously unavailable to the public, such as unreported clinical trial data, internal memos, etc.

What I learned is that, typically, one in four patients feels worse when beginning any antidepressant drug and "drops out" or quits use of the drug within the first month; almost half quit within three months. That is to say that while antidepressant drugs may help some people, they are not reliable, not even close.

That might not be such a problem if drug companies were straight up about this, but that wouldn't be good for sales. On the contrary, doctors are instructed, through industry propaganda, to "reduce" patient drop-out by "managing" the side effects and encouraging patients to stick with the program rather than encouraging physicians to listen to patients' individual sensitivities.

Perhaps if Tooker's doctor had been better informed about the adverse reaction of agitation, Tooker would be alive today. Instead, his doctor repeatedly upped the dosage and prescribed a tranquilizer to calm his agitation.

Agitation Is a Common Side Effect

Agitation is a very common side effect of antidepressant drugs, primarily during the early stages of treatment or shortly after a change in dosage (up or down). Extreme agitation is known as akathisia, an internal unrest, turmoil or torture.

In clinical trials for SSRIs (the most commonly prescribed family of antidepressants), this reaction has been well-recognized and documented since the early '80s. Prozac's own clinical trials, prior to its launch in 1988 and post-launch, recorded rates of agitation and akathisia from between five and 25 percent.

Patients are twice as likely to attempt suicide on antidepressants as on sugar pills.

Conservatively speaking then, one in 20 patients becomes agitated on antidepressant drugs—five percent is a significant adverse reaction that doctors need to be informed about and need to warn patients about, but they generally don't. The concern is that agitation is a very potent predictor of suicide and violence.

By extrapolating from clinical trial data and multiplying by numbers of users, Dr. David Healy claims that one in 500 users of antidepressant drugs will complete suicide because of the drug. That's 100,000 tragic and unnecessary deaths.

Clearly, drug companies have a lot to lose if this information becomes well understood, since there are 40 to 50 million people world wide on antidepressant drugs and the number is growing—there was an 80 percent increase in antidepressant prescriptions in Canada from 1999 to 2004.

In February 2005, an incredible study authored by Dr. Dean Fergusson was published in the *British Medical Journal.* Dr. Fergusson is a scientist with the Ottawa Health Research Institute and teaches in the Department of Medicine at the University of Ottawa. His meta-analysis reviewed data on 90,000 patients from some 700 clinical trials. His team found that patients are twice as likely to attempt suicide on antidepressants as on sugar pills. This result confirmed other study results of 2000 and 2001.

Huh? Patients are put on antidepressant drugs to lower suicide risk, not double it!

Little Evidence that Antidepressants Help

Just how effective are antidepressants in relieving symptoms of depression? Incredibly, there is little evidence that antidepressant drugs actually produce benefits. We know that they may help some people in the short term, but over the long term we find a worsening of depression or anxiety compared to placebo-treated patients. Too often, new and more severe psychiatric symptoms are triggered by the drug itself, such as drug-induced manic or psychotic attacks, which just means more drugs to counter those symptoms, and so on. For everyone helped by a drug treatment, there may be another harmed.

And then there's the disturbing and very real issue of dependence on antidepressants. When you try to stop taking these drugs, you can suffer an emotionally-distressing withdrawal that includes "crashing" with depression, fatigue and feelings of hopelessness, and often involves painful physical symptoms such as flu-like syndrome, muscle cramps and shock-like headaches.

A causal relationship between antidepressants and suicide has been established since the early '80s; why did it take until 2004 before regulatory agencies requested of drug companies that they warn consumers and physicians? How many people needlessly died in that time? How many are still to die?

Light a Candle

Clearly it's better to light a candle than curse the darkness. With intelligence and integrity, and with the intention of patient safety rather than profit motive, we can save lives. With compassion and skill—and a dose of generosity—each of us can reach out to those we love during their dark times. We must. It will come back to us in spades. We're all making a difference. We all can change the world.

The last word goes to Tooker: "We can do it. If we will it."

Should Physicians Help Terminally Ill Patients Commit Suicide?

Chapter Preface

Oregon is the only state in the country that allows legal physician-assisted suicide (PAS). State voters approved the measure in 1994 and overwhelmingly voted three years later not to repeal it. Oregon statutory law permits physicians to prescribe a lethal dose of medication to a patient agreed by two doctors to be within six months of dying from an incurable condition. In January 2006, the United States Supreme Court, in *Gonzales v Oregon*, ruled that the U.S. Attorney General could not enforce the federal Controlled Substance Act against physicians prescribing drugs for the assisted suicide of the terminally ill as permitted by Oregon law.

The Death-with-Dignity Act allows terminally ill Oregon citizens to obtain and use prescriptions from their doctors for self-administered, lethal medications. Although the law legalizes PAS, it specifically prohibits euthanasia, where a doctor or other person directly administers a medication to end another's life. To request a prescription for lethal medications, the Death-with-Dignity Act requires that a patient must be:

- An adult,

- An Oregonian,

- Capable of making and communicating health care decisions, and

- Diagnosed as terminally ill with less than six months to live.

The Oregon Department of Human Services is statutorily required to collect information regarding compliance with the act and to make the information available to the general public on an annual basis. During the years 1998 through 2005, 246 Oregonians took lethal medications. Although males and females have been equally likely to take advantage of the

Death-with-Dignity Act, in several ways PAS patients differed from Oregonians dying from the same underlying diseases. For example, PAS patients were older and more apt to be divorced or never married than married and widowed residents. A higher level of education has been strongly associated with the use of PAS. Oregonians with a B.A. degree or higher were nearly eight times more likely to use PAS than those without a high school diploma. In contrast, several groups were less likely to use PAS. These include individuals eighty-five years of age or older, people who did not graduate from high school, people who are married or widowed, and residents living east of the Cascade Range, the mountainous region that runs north-south from British Columbia through Oregon to Northern California.

The Oregon Department of Human Services also reported that physicians indicated that patient requests for lethal medications resulted from multiple end-of-life concerns in 2005. Eighty percent of all patients had at least three concerns. The most frequently mentioned were: a decreasing ability to participate in activities that made life enjoyable (89 percent), loss of dignity (89 percent), and loss of autonomy (79 percent). These findings are very similar to those in a study of Oregon hospice nurses and social workers caring for PAS patients.

All Lives Do Not Have Equal Worth

Eric Cohen and Leon R. Kass

About the authors: *Eric Cohen is the director of the program in biotechnology and American democracy at the Ethics and Public Policy Center. Leon R. Kass is a professor in the Committee on Social Thought at the University of Chicago.*

Death and dying are once again subjects of intense public attention. During his confirmation hearings, [U.S. Supreme Court] Chief Justice John Roberts was grilled about his views on removing life-sustaining treatments from debilitated patients and warned by various liberal Senators not to interfere with the "right to die." In California and Vermont, state legislators are working to legalize assisted suicide, while the Bush administration is trying to restrict the practice by prohibiting doctors from using federally-controlled narcotics to end their patients' lives. . . .

Although growing old is a natural part of being human, the circumstances in which most Americans age and die are increasingly "unnatural" and surely unprecedented. Longer life expectancies and lower birth rates lead to the graying of society; smaller and less stable families weaken the ties that bind. Death comes on the doctor's watch and in high-tech surroundings, almost always following years of chronic illness, typically preceded by decisions about further medical intervention, increasingly made on behalf of patients incapable of making decisions for themselves. Caregivers often do not know how to honor those who have lost their most human qualities. Thanks to medicine's prowess in sustaining life on the edge, it is harder than ever to know when it is "time to die."

Eric Cohen and Leon R. Kass, "Cast Me Not Off in Old Age," *Commentary*, vol. 121, January 2006.

The Approaching Perfect Storm

The miseries of aging and decline were hardly unknown to our ancestors, and are eloquently attested in the biblical plea from which we have taken our title. When asked if he would choose to live over again, Thomas Jefferson said yes, but only between ages twenty-five and sixty. Thereafter, he wrote, "the powers of life are sensibly on the wane, sight becomes dim, hearing dull, memory constantly enlarging its frightful blank and parting with all we have ever seen or known, spirits evaporate, bodily debility creeps on palsying every limb, and so faculty after faculty quits us, and where then is life?" Yet in Jefferson's time, most people never reached this extended period of debility, because they died suddenly in the nursery of life or at the peak of their flourishing. Living to old age was the dream of the vulnerable many; living with old age was the problem of the fortunate few.

Roughly 40 percent of deaths in the United States are now preceded by a period of enfeeblement, debility, and (often) dementia lasting up to a decade.

In developed societies today, by contrast, old age is the norm. Average life expectancy in the United States is now seventy-eight years and rising (up from forty-seven in 1900), and those over age eighty-five are already the fastest growing segment of the population. People are not only living longer; they are staying healthier well into their sixties, seventies, and eighties, and they expect to enjoy many years of vigorous retirement. On balance, it is a wonderful time to be old, and the democratization and expansion of old age are among modernity's greatest achievements.

Yet the coming of the mass geriatric society is also a source of tremendous anxiety. Americans worry about the soaring costs of Social Security and Medicare, the collapse of private pensions, the shortage of good nursing homes, and the potential clash between the young and the old over resources and priorities. Our deepest worries are personal: we dread spending our final years in a degraded state, resented by caregivers or abandoned by loved ones, of little use to ourselves, never mind to others.

Such worries are not unjustified. Although most Americans can expect to live healthily well past sixty-five, many will also live long enough to endure a prolonged period of frailty. According to a recent Rand study, roughly 40 percent of deaths in the United States are now preceded by a period of enfeeblement, debility, and (often) dementia lasting up to a decade. Prominent are those suffering from Alzheimer's disease, a condition that steadily destroys the mind and body, strips individuals of self-awareness and self-control, and often requires that they spend their final years in an institution, incapable of feeding or bathing themselves or of using a toilet. Today, over 4 million Americans suffer from Alzheimer's; by mid-century, that number is expected to rise to over 13 million—all of them requiring many years of extensive, expensive, and exhausting full-time care.

[Some] believe that the indignities of old age—especially dementia—belie all sanctimonious talk of "equal worth."

Yet precisely as the need is rising, the pool of available family caregivers is dwindling. Families are smaller, less stable, and more geographically spread out. Most women are now employed outside the home. The well-to-do can afford to hire professionals, but there are already shortages of geriatricians and nurses. Those jobs requiring great humanity but offering little paid reward—like feeding Alzheimer's patients or changing bedpans—are greatly undersubscribed.

All this creates a perfect social storm. As the number of retired baby-boomers expands, they will seek to augment existing social programs for the elderly, creating novel fiscal challenges for Medicare and Medicaid. Politically, long-term-care benefits might become the sequel to prescription-drug benefits—and far costlier. At the same time, the burdens of caring for needy elders will test the strength of already fragile modern families. Those in middle age may wonder about the wisdom (or duty) of sacrificing so much, for so long, on behalf of lives that seem so diminished. And they may come to believe that the death of the elderly is preferable to life in what seems like such a miserable condition. . . .

Do All People Have Equal Worth?

Until now, our society has been largely spared such questions. And when they have been raised, usually in private, we have had solid moral answers, backed by our religious and political traditions as well as by the venerable teachings of medical ethics. When it comes to the right to life and human care, most Americans are committed—at least in the abstract—to the view that all human beings are "created equal." And since the days of Hippocrates, physicians for their part have eschewed judging the worth of the lives they treat and have refused "to give a deadly drug if asked" or even "to make a suggestion to that effect." Never are the disabled deemed unworthy of medical or humane care; on the contrary, their need for care is precisely the reason we are obliged to provide it. . . .

This general agreement regarding equal human worth can disappear in certain cases. Although many continue to believe that every human life, regardless of debility, possesses equal dignity, others now argue openly that equal treatment for all is best advanced by not diverting precious resources to the severely disabled. Still others believe that the indignities of old age—especially dementia—belie all sanctimonious talk of "equal worth."

Among these people are the advocates of euthanasia or mercy killing. For the time being, America seems immune to embracing this particular "solution" to the burdens of an aging society. Even in those states—like California and Vermont—that have considered joining Oregon in legalizing assisted suicide, the justification is "personal choice," not a category of human beings officially defined by hospitals or the state as "life unworthy of living" or "better off dead." At the same time, however, more and more commentators are deploring the amount of money spent on medical care for people near the end of life. As the American population ages, we can expect to hear even more talk of people with "low quality of life," unworthy of the resources "wasted" on them. What begins today as a campaign to give individuals a right to ease themselves out of life can easily turn into a campaign to get the enfeebled and demented to exercise their "right to die," or, since they are unable to do the deadly deed themselves, to "exercise it for them."

Against this danger, the assertion that "life is sacred and should always be sustained" will prove an insufficient defense. Indeed, even those who pledge their belief in the sanctity of every human being will often wonder whether intervening medically really benefits the life they hold to be so precious. Is it love or is it cruelty, for instance, to cure the pneumonia in an elderly person suffering from a painful form of terminal cancer—especially one so demented that the mitigating comforts of family and friendship cannot be appreciated? Is it love or is it cruelty to extend a life marked by incontinence of bladder and bowel, uncontrollable outbursts of rage, or psychophysical misery caused by Alzheimer's? Is it love or is it cruelty to force a patient with mild dementia to continue kidney dialysis that he vigorously resists, knowing that he cannot understand either how the dialysis can help him or that ceasing treatment will bring imminent death? Faced with these painful choices, and in moments of weakness, hastening death's arrival may seem the compassionate thing to do.

Traditional Medical Ethics

Traditional medical ethics, ever mindful of this temptation, has been very clear about the duty to resist it: never to kill, always to care. If doctors and others are faithfully to benefit the life the patient still has, they cannot sit in ultimate judgment of its worth, and cannot ever think that lethal intervention is an acceptable "therapeutic option." This holds true even for those (non-demented) patients who knowingly ask doctors or family members to help them die—whether in the present because they are suffering now, or in the future because they cannot bear the thought of living with dementia.

Here then is the most poignant dilemma faced by caregivers: not wishing to condemn the worth of people's lives, yet not wanting to bind them to the rack of their growing misery.

But traditional medical ethics has also long taught that benefiting the life a debilitated person still has does not mean taking every possible medical action to extend it. Senescence leads inevitably to death, medicine or no medicine. And so, while "active killing" may be incompatible with true caregiving, "letting die" is always part of it. In this reasoning, life-sustaining treatment may be—and often should be—forgone or terminated if the interventions themselves impose undue burdens on the patient or interfere with the comfortable death of someone irretrievably dying. Guidance in this area comes from distinguishing between the burdens of a treatment (imposed by caregivers and for which they are thus responsible) and the burdens of living with a terrible disease (imposed by nature and for which they are not responsible).

Yet as we enter the mass geriatric society, it is clear that our new technological capacities are putting pressure on these sensible distinctions. A century ago, Dr. William Osler could write: "Pneumonia may well be called the friend of the aged. Taken off by it in an acute, short, not often painful illness, the old man escapes these cold gradations of decay so distressing to himself and to his friends." Today, thanks to antibiotics, the aged have no natural friends—or few that are not more commonly regarded as enemies. Life-sustaining intervention if effective and not especially burdensome, have come to be regarded as standard care and morally obligatory. As a result, well-meaning and morally sound decisions to treat intervening illnesses . . . can make us complicit in the continuing miseries and degradations of those we love.

Here then is the most poignant dilemma faced by caregivers: not wishing to condemn the worth of people's lives, yet not wanting to bind them to the rack of their growing misery; not wishing to say they are better off dead, yet not wanting always to oppose their going hither. Under these circumstances, with no simple formulas for finding the best course of action, individuals and families must find their way, case by case and moment to moment, often with only unattractive options to choose from and knowing that whatever path they choose, they will feel the weight of the path not chosen.

Aging Is Not a Private Matter

Even if the burdens of aging and death are always borne most fully by individuals and families, how we age and die are not only private matters. Our communal practices and social policies shape the environments in which aging and caregiving take place—not only in moments of crisis, when life-or-death decisions need to be made, but in the long days of struggle and everyday attendance. Faith-based institutions and community groups support families in meeting those needs they cannot meet alone. Programs like Medicaid assist those who are old and impoverished, in need of nursing that they cannot themselves afford.

In the years ahead, this need for social supports will only increase, especially if we are to fight the temptation to turn caregiving entirely into a state responsibility. Affordable insurance, respite relief for caregivers, reliable and reimbursable home services, technologies to assist in giving basic bodily care—all these and more can enhance the economic and social supports of those coping with extended debility. Recruitment of volunteers to aid in eldercare is a perfect objective for the many groups, both liberal and conservative, interested in promoting civic engagement and renewing civil society.

We live already in a world in which the life cycle has largely lost its ethical meaning.

But we cannot pretend that individual families, or society as a whole, will have unlimited resources, particularly in a populace with more elderly persons and fewer young workers. Americans will need to make hard choices among competing goods, and to confront the limits of even our own affluent society. And even then the biggest challenges before us will not be economic in nature but cultural and spiritual—how to deepen our understanding of what it means to age and die, how to combat the overly medicalized view of old age that now dominates our attitudes and our institutions, how to recover the wisdom contained in the human life cycle.

As we noted earlier, Americans increasingly regard old age as a bundle of needs and problems demanding solution, or as a time of life whose meaning is defined largely by the struggle to stay healthy and fit. This outlook has generated discontent with the life cycle itself, producing an insatiable desire for more and more medical miracles, and creating the fantasy that we can transcend our limitations—or that death itself may be pushed back indefinitely. More deeply, this same outlook has engendered the illusion that independence is the whole truth about our lives, causing us to undervalue those attachments and obligations that bind and complete us.

We live already in a world in which the life cycle has largely lost its ethical meaning. Aware as we may be that we are on a solitary journey that ends inevitably in the grave, few of us take our bearings from nature's eternal teaching that there is a

127

time to be born and a time to die. We learn little from the rhythm of growth and decay, everything in its season, our own finitude transcended and redeemed by generation upon generation of new birth and renewal, transforming each singular finite trajectory into a permanently recurring cycle of life.

This cultural myopia is no trivial matter. Indeed, in the mass geriatric society it could have deadly consequences. For unless we learn to accept both our frailties and our finitude, we are likely to find the burdens of caregiving intolerable. And unless we learn how to let loved ones die when the time comes, we will be tempted to kill—self-righteously, of course, in the guise of a false compassion. Sooner or later, when the medical gospel of healthy aging and the legal gospel of living wills are shown to have been false teachings, we may easily fall prey to the utilitarian gospel of euthanasia, whose prophets are patiently waiting in the wings for their time upon our cultural stage. Paradoxically, a dogmatic insistence that patients must be kept alive regardless of the depth of their disabilities—that severe dementia or unmanageable suffering deserves no consideration in deciding when to "let nature take its course"—may only make mercy killing appear to be the more compassionate remedy for the miseries of extended decline.

In the end, there is no "solution" to the problems of old age, at least no solution that any civilized society could tolerate. But there are better and worse ways to see our aging condition. The better way begins in thinking of ourselves less as wholly autonomous individuals than as members of families; in relinquishing our mistaken belief that medicine can miraculously liberate our loved ones or ourselves from debility and decline, and instead taking up our role as caregivers; and in abjuring the fantasy that we can control the manner and the hour of our dying, learning instead to accept death in its proper season as mortal beings replaced and renewed by the generations that follow.

The Phrase "Culture of Life" Is Meaningless

Anna Quindlen

About the author: *Anna Quindlen is a best-selling novelist and a columnist for the* New York Times *and* Newsweek.

P lease, I imagine myself saying to the editor, don't put that picture of her on the cover. Use the picture from years ago, the one in which she is wearing the print blouse, her hair long, her dark eyes stars behind spiky lashes. She looks shy and somehow pleased with herself, slender and pretty and perhaps aware of both facts. Use that picture.

But of course no one will know who that woman is. It is the other face people will recognize, the mouth agape, the eyes glittering but oddly fixed, the hair cropped and androgynous, the antithesis of the girl with light in her eyes.

That heartbreaking second photo is the Terri Schiavo people have seen. An eating disorder may have brought on the heart failure that left her in a persistent vegetative state 15 years ago, yet a young woman so conscious of her appearance has been exposed to all the world in pitiful infirmity. It is a shame that anyone released those images. She should have been remembered for what she was, not what's left of her.

We all know the story now. A raft of doctors said over the years that Terri's reactions were purely reflexive, that she would not recover, that she would never be more than the vessel in which her spirit once lived, like a music box that no longer plays. The courts ruled over and over again that her husband had the right to withdraw a feeding tube in deference to what he said were the expressed wishes of his wife. Her parents objected. Congress passed legislation, spitting in the face of the

courts—as well as states' rights and the separation of powers—but even the last-ditch federal jurists had the strength to
uphold the law.

Culture of Life

Arguments about Terri's case centered on something described
as a "culture of life." It is an empty suit of a phrase, absent an
individual to give it shape. There is no culture of life. There is
the culture of your life, and the culture of mine. There is what
each of us considers bearable, and what we will not bear.
There are those of us who believe that under certain conditions the cruelest thing you can do to people you love is to
force them to live. There are those of us who define living not
by whether the heart beats and the lungs lift but whether the
spirit is there, whether the music box plays.

---

*No public official is going to tell me how to xoxo [show
love for] my sister.*

There are two different opinions about what the culture of
her own life meant to Terri Schiavo. Her husband, Michael,
insisted that, like many other Americans, she expressed a
strong wish not to be kept alive by extraordinary measures.
Her parents said they did not believe that was true, that they
wanted her feeding tube kept in and her care transferred to
them. One measure of how topsy-turvy this story became was
the constant suggestion that Terri's husband should simply ac-
cede to the desires of his in-laws, as though that would be a
good thing instead of a gutless betrayal. My own husband
knows that I never want artificial means to keep me alive.
What an insult to my memory and our marriage it would be
if he opted out when the going got rough and permitted others to salve their heartbreak by maintaining a shadow of my
self.

There are many ways in which this case has been divvied up in public. Spouse vs. parents. Liberals vs. conservatives. Secular vs. religious. But it is truly about that thing that defines free human beings: the right to self-determination instead of a one-size-fits-all approach in private matters, in those issues that take place in bedrooms and kitchens and hospices. It's a primal demand for a personal sense of control in the face of intrusive government, intrusive medicine and intrusive strangers who think holding a crucifix like a blunt instrument makes them righteous when it really only makes them sanctimonious.

Our Own Definition of Life

Last week my father and I received this short e-mail from my sister, a public-school teacher in San Francisco:

> i'm telling you both this now if i am ever in a 'persistent veg-etative state' please let me die do not have a feeding tube put in me and in no uncertain terms: do not let the united states government get involved. xoxo

No public official is going to tell me how to *xoxo* my sister. No church, no court. The Schiavo case has asked us to look at our own definition of life, not at some formless notion cobbled out of the Bible, medical textbooks and impersonal sentiment. My sister's throaty laugh, her prodigious knowledge of history, her garrulous nature: that's the true picture of her, the one with the light in her eyes. She's counting on me to make certain that image is not replaced by something empty and depleted. She's counting on me to safeguard her dignity and her humanity, which are one and the same.

Many of us feel the way she does. Once the feeding tube was removed, polls showed that the majority of Americans believed Terri Schiavo should be allowed to die. That's probably because they've been there. They are the true judges and lawmakers and priests. They've been at the bedside, watching someone they love in agony as cancer nipped at the spine, as the chest rose and fell with the cruel mimicry of the respirator, as the music of personality dwindled to a single note and then fell silent. They know life when they see it, and they know it when it is gone.

The Legality of Oregon's Physician-Assisted Suicide Law Is a Victory for Patients and Doctors

Mark Taylor

About the author*: Mark Taylor covers legal affairs, including fraud and abuse, tax, antitrust, and compliance issues for Modern Healthcare.*

Last week's decision by the U.S. Supreme Court to uphold Oregon's controversial assisted-suicide law gave a boost to the rights of physicians, patients and states in the battle over how much say the federal government has in regulating healthcare.

The Supreme Court's Jan. 17 decision was a rebuke of the Bush administration's attempt to use federal drug laws to overrule a state law allowing physician-assisted suicide.

Though most healthcare players generally opposed Oregon's law or remained neutral, and physicians did not present a unified front in Oregon's battle to allow physician-assisted suicide, many doctors were eager to keep the federal government from expanding its role in the physician-patient relationship.

Impact of Court Decision

The court's decision "removes a dark shadow hanging over all Oregon physicians delivering end-of-life care," said Peter Rasmussen, a Portland physician board certified in medical oncology and palliative care who has assisted in more than a dozen patient deaths under the law.

Mark Taylor, "A Matter of Life or Death; By Upholding an Assisted-Suicide Law, the Supreme Court Helps Reinforce the Rights of Doctors, Patients and the States," *Modern Healthcare*, vol. 36, January 23, 2006. Copyright 2006 Crain Communications, Inc. Reproduced by permission.

"The Bush administration would have had members of their organization deciding what was and wasn't legitimate medical treatment. If it stood, it could have gone far beyond end-of-life care to reproductive care and stem-cell research. They could have used their ethics to track down and punish doctors," he said. Rasmussen said the court restated the principle that the regulation of medicine resides within the states.

Also, the ruling gives further insulation to the physician-patient relationship. The Supreme Court decision grants greater autonomy to physicians and protects them from government prosecution and civil lawsuits, said Stuart Gerson, a former Justice Department official now with the law firm Epstein, Becker & Green. "It strengthens the physician-patient relationship and pulls the government out of this kind of decisionmaking, while reiterating that the federal government can't supersede state law," Gerson said.

By a 6–3 majority, the court held that [U.S. Attorney General John] Ashcroft exceeded his authority under the Controlled Substances Act and could not punish doctors who helped patients to die by prescribing lethal doses of drugs.

Patients' rights advocates also applauded the ruling. "This restores the common understanding that the federal government has no business at the bedside of dying patients," said Barbara Coombs Lee, president and co-chief executive officer of Compassion & Choices, a national organization advocating better end-of-life care. "This tells states that they can establish aid in dying as a legal alternative. It lifts the cloud of uncertainty over state legislatures about whether they have the authority to do this. They do have the authority as well as the moral obligation. Dying patients want this right, this control, this choice, this hope."

Oregons PAS Law

The Supreme Court's ruling was the result of a move by former U.S. Attorney General John Ashcroft, who in 2001 challenged the Oregon law by issuing a rule that said dispensing controlled substances to assist a suicide was "not a legitimate medical practice" and violated the 1970 Controlled Substances Act. Ashcroft said that a 1971 regulation within that law gives the attorney general authority to regulate physician prescription activity, and deny, suspend or revoke physician registration for activities "inconsistent with the public interest."

The state of Oregon, along with a physician, pharmacist and several patients, challenged Ashcroft's rule in 2001 and a federal district court prevented its enforcement. The 9th U.S. Circuit Court of Appeals struck down the rule, saying it violated the balance between states and the federal government. The attorney general appealed that ruling to the U.S. Supreme Court, which heard arguments last year and released its decision last week.

Had the attorney general-led effort succeeded, the effect would have been to restrict the use of powerful drugs in physician-assisted suicides. Since the law's implementation in 1997, 208 Oregonians have requested physician assistance in dying.

But by a 6–3 majority, the court held that Ashcroft exceeded his authority under the Controlled Substances Act and could not punish doctors who helped patients to die by prescribing lethal doses of drugs. Writing the majority opinion, Justice Anthony Kennedy said that, "The authority claimed by the attorney general is both beyond his expertise and incongruous with the statutory purposes and design."

Justice Antonin Scalia, writing for the dissenting minority, said using the federal commerce power to "prevent physician-assisted suicide is unquestionably permissible."

Physicians Opposed to PAS

While Oregon voters have supported physician-assisted suicide, there remains significant opposition from doctors nationally, and more than one-third of Oregon doctors in a recent survey opposed it. Many have united against the practice. Retired radiation oncologist Kenneth Stevens, vice president of Portland, Ore.–based Physicians for Compassionate Care, said his organization was disappointed in the Supreme Court's decision, although he noted that the ruling was made on a narrow legal point and did not speak to the legality of the state's assisted-suicide law. Stevens said opponents of the law plan nothing new in that state, but said his organization will continue to speak out against what he calls the harms and dangers of the practice.

Stevens said he didn't think the Supreme Court decision would encourage passage of assisted-suicide laws in other states. "We were told after the Oregon law passed, it would sweep the country, but it has not passed in any other state since," said the retired faculty member of the Oregon Health & Sciences University.

Opponents of the law, such as Stevens, said some patients feel particularly vulnerable under the law. "The people who have requested this have not chosen suicide for uncontrollable pain, but for mostly social and psychological reasons. They don't want to lose control over their lives and become dependent. And this strikes fear in people with disabilities who fear subtle pressures for them to end their own lives."

Healthcare lawyer Gerson also said the court's decision is troubling in some ways. "It overlooks questions of patient competence in making these decisions and doesn't touch on the role of doctors in making the decision to die."

Other opponents to the Oregon law offered similar reasoning. The American Medical Association has opposed physician-assisted suicide in its policies and public statements, but declined to comment on the Supreme Court decision. The

AMA policy explains that physician-assisted suicide is "inconsistent with the physician's professional role," saying that dying patients should be provided aggressive comfort-care measures and a greater reliance on hospice care. Requests for assisted suicide indicate "that the patient's needs are unmet."

"Physicians must not perform euthanasia or participate in physician-assisted suicide," the policy reads.

While the Oregon Medical Association also opposed the Oregon law, the OMA objected to what it viewed as a flaw in the law and has remained neutral on the concept of physician-assisted suicide.

Hospitals and Insurers Were Neutral

Hospitals and insurers have mostly chosen to stay out of the fray.

The Oregon Association of Hospitals and Health Systems remained neutral because its members were divided on the issue, said Gwen Dayton, executive vice president and general counsel. Dayton said because the law remained intact throughout the legal challenges to it, the Supreme Court ruling should have little impact on Oregon providers.

"I can imagine though, that some physicians may have held off participating due to the uncertainty created by the challenge to the law," Dayton said. "Had the decision gone the other way, it would not (have) impacted hospitals much because very few assisted suicides have occurred in hospitals."

Stevens said hospitals have mostly stayed out of the debate, although he noted that Seattle-based Providence Health System, one of the largest systems in Oregon operated by a Roman Catholic religious order, has spoken out against the law and the practice. Providence didn't return phone calls seeking comment.

Angela Hult, a spokeswoman for Regence Blue Cross and Blue Shield of Oregon, the state's largest health plan, said the industry took no position on the law and her company didn't either. She said she's uncertain how many physicians have billed the 1 million-member Blues plan for reimbursement for physician-assisted suicide. "I don't think we have any code for it. If it's billed at all, it's probably for a routine consultation."

Rasmussen, the doctor, said that the vast majority of physician-assisted deaths occur in patient homes, nursing homes or hospices. He said pain is typically not the reason cited by most patients requesting physician assistance in dying. "We're so good at controlling the pain, that's not usually the issue. It's nausea, shortness of breath, incontinence and symptoms of being increasingly dependent on others," he said. "They are having family members observe this and don't want them to exhaust themselves emotionally and financially. The thing they have in common is they are usually very self-reliant and have taken responsibility for themselves and valued retaining that control all of their lives."

Democrats Have Become the Party of Euthanasia

Ramesh Ponnuru

About the author: *Ramesh Ponnuru is a senior editor for the National Review, a politically conservative magazine.*

It was easy to forget, during the weeks in March 2005 when the controversy over Terri Schiavo filled the airwaves, that assisted suicide is illegal in Florida—as it is in every state but Oregon (where it is legal for the terminally ill). The debate on television, on op-ed pages, and in the Congress often seemed to center on whether Florida law was wise to give her husband Michael Schiavo the right to make the life-or-death decision.

Michael Schiavo wanted Terri Schiavo's feeding and hydration tube to be removed so that she would die. He claimed that this action would be in keeping with her wishes. His evidence for this claim consisted of two statements. Michael Schiavo's brother, Scott, said that she had told him that she did not want to be on life support the way Michael and Scott's grandmother had been. "If I ever go like that, just let me go," she had supposedly said. Terri's sister-in-law Joan Schiavo said that the two had watched a TV movie about a man on a feeding tube and that Terri had said, "No tubes for me."

Terri's siblings and parents, the Schindlers, did not believe that she would have had those wishes. They thought it suspicious that Michael Schiavo and his relatives remembered these alleged wishes only in 1997, seven years after her incapacitation. They had not mentioned them in 1992, when Michael Schiavo sued doctors for negligence in Schiavo's treatment and, in the course of his suit, promised to spend the rest of his life taking care of her with the proceeds of the suit. (He won a $1.1 million settlement.) Nor did they mention them in 1994, when Schiavo and the Schindlers clashed in court over whether Terri should be treated for an infection.

The Schindlers considered Michael to have abandoned Terri upon having children with and becoming engaged to another woman. They also contested the diagnosis, crucial to the case for withdrawing the tube under Florida law, that Terri was in a "persistent vegetative state." Their lawyers produced experts who said that she was actually "minimally conscious."

Florida courts sided with Michael Schiavo. For years, as appeals were filed, the case became a low-profile cause for pro-lifers. The (Republican) state legislature in Florida had tried to intervene in favor of the Schindlers but were rebuffed by the courts. In the spring of 2005, when the Schindlers' appeals began to run out and permanent withdrawal of the tube looked imminent, the dispute began to draw national attention. Congress tried in various ways to force federal courts to consider the issue anew.

Pro-lifers failed to challenge the notion that it is acceptable to kill those who wish to be killed.

At first, congressional support for intervention was bipartisan and, indeed, nearly unanimous. Many congressmen had misgivings about whether Terri's wishes were really being respected. Calling for a new hearing seemed like a modest step to many. And, perhaps most important, the only voters really paying attention to the case in the beginning were pro-lifers and disability-rights activists who opposed the killing of Terri Schiavo. There seemed to be no political downside to stepping in.

That changed within days. The public reacted strongly against the intervention. Many people favored the removal of the tube. Others thought that Congress should stay out of the dispute. Even some pro-life conservatives, perhaps unaware that the Supreme Court had already gotten the federal government deeply involved in the issue, wondered whether it was appropriate for the feds to undo the judgments of Florida courts. Still others recoiled from the whole awful tragedy and its exploitation by the media and politicians. They wanted it off their screens.

The liberal intelligentsia, seeing that a majority was with them, expressed a kind of gleeful fury about the case. They were pushing on an open door since, pro-lifers barely made the principled argument against euthanasia. For understandable political and legal reasons, those who wanted to keep feeding Terri emphasized that it was not clear that she was in a "persistent vegetative state." But in so doing, they let the notion that it is acceptable for people who are in that state to be starved to death slide right by. It made tactical sense to question whether Mrs. Schiavo really would have wanted to die this way. But in asking it, pro-lifers failed to challenge the notion that it is acceptable to kill those who wish to be killed.

The concept of the "sanctity of life" was a spectral presence in the debate, never given a rational form. So it was easy for people to fall into the assumption that it was an essentially religious concept. Proponents of feeding Mrs. Schiavo were, by and large, Christians, and Christian conservatives at that. They often claimed, or implied, that they were doing God's will. Resisting euthanasia thus came to be seen as somehow theocratic, and irrational. Pro-lifers were "emot[ing] with bug-eyed religiosity," the Financial Times calmly opined. Hendrik Hertzberg called them "Christianists" in The New Yorker, a label that implicitly (and with malice aforethought) compared them to bin Laden and his followers.

It cannot be denied that pro-lifers were guilty of some excesses. Some of them, on the basis of very little evidence, accused Michael Schiavo of having caused his wife's collapse through abuse. They should have refrained from that kind of charge (which ended up backfiring anyway). Yet one need not excuse such conduct to see that the portrayal of pro-lifers as categorically irrational turned matters upside down. There is a perfectly rational case against euthanasia. The case *for* it, on the other hand, almost inescapably rests on what might be described as a kind of irrational spirituality.

The case against starts, once again, with the idea that human beings have inherent worth and dignity, and therefore are equal in fundamental rights, simply by virtue of being human. The right to life has to be among these rights, which means that it cannot depend on race, or age, or health, or sex. It cannot depend even on whether the person who has it wants it: He doesn't cease to be a human being with the full complement of rights simply because he wants to die. (It is because the right is intrinsic to human beings that it is also inalienable, as our Founders, who were not theocrats, put it.)

For the law to allow people to take innocent human lives—even their own—is necessarily for it to join the party of death in regarding some lives as not worth living.

The alternative view is that some human beings have the right not to be killed on the basis of qualities that they, in particular, have: for example, the immediately exercisable capacity for conceptual thinking or other types of mental activity. If that quality is what confers the right to life, then abortion, embryo-destructive research, and the euthanasia of the permanently comatose or persistently vegetative are all acceptable. But since human mental capacity varies continuously, we will have to identify a non-arbitrary minimum level necessary to possess rights, and then explain why people who have more of that quality should not be regarded as greater in worth and dignity than people who have less of it. It is impossible to do either.

Thus it ends up being impossible to confine the category of lives deemed unworthy of protection to the unborn and the persistently vegetative—impossible not just practically, but in principle. We have seen how this works at the beginning of life: Whether our criterion is the ability to reason, self-awareness, or the capacity to experience pain, newborn infants do not differ from late-term fetuses. Pro-choicers who find [the utilitarian philosopher] Peter Singer's advocacy of infanticide repulsive cannot come up with a persuasive argument for why he is wrong. He differs from them only in his willingness to embrace the logical consequences of the premises he joins them in affirming.

For the law to allow people to take innocent human lives—even their own—is necessarily for it to join the party of death in regarding some lives as not worth living. This is perhaps especially true when the law restricts the "right" to commit suicide to specific categories of people, such as the severely disabled and ill. As bioethics writer Eric Cohen noted in *The Weekly Standard*, at least one Florida appeals court that considered the Schiavo case made this move without even realizing it. It simply assumed that the only reason anyone—including Mrs. Schiavo herself, or rather the Mrs. Schiavo of the past looking at the situation—could want to keep the tube connected was the possibility that "a miracle would somehow recreate" her cerebrum. It assumed, that is, that Mrs. Schiavo would not have wanted to continue living indefinitely in a persistent vegetative state, because no one would. It was all right to end her life, that is, because it was, objectively, not a life worth living.

Mrs. Schiavo was commonly described as "brain dead." [The author] Christopher Hitchens used the Schiavo controversy as the occasion for another of his denunciations of "religious fanatics": "The end of the brain, or the replacement of the brain by a liquefied and shrunken void, is . . . if not the absolute end of 'life,' the unarguable conclusion of human life.

It disqualifies the victim from any further say in human affairs." Mrs. Schiavo, he writes, was already Michael Schiavo's "ex-wife" before the tube was pulled.

Hitchens's statement, taken literally, is truer than he appears to realize. Most people accept brain-death as the criterion for death. But the prevailing standard has required the death of the whole brain, not just the cerebrum. The person must not only lack higher mental functions, that is, but have ceased to exist as an organism. Hitchens was moving the goalposts: treating people without higher mental functions as expendable by redefining them as already dead.

The argument that allowing euthanasia violates a basic human right, denies the ground of human equality, and would also in principle require acceptance of evils that almost everyone can recognize as such corresponds, in its conclusions, with the Judeo-Christian tradition. But it does not at any point rely on the premise that God is a Trinity, or that He even exists, or that the pope or the church can teach infallibly in moral matters.

The argument *for* euthanasia, however, often seems to depend on a kind of superstition: on a dualism that separates a person from his body. This dualism holds a person, understood as a consciousness, to be important and worth protecting, but does not so hold the physical organism that this person merely "inhabits." The person is the "ghost in the machine" or, to use [novelist] Anna Quindlen's more recent metaphor, the tune in the music box. Libertarian commentator Glenn Reynolds took this valorization of the willing, desiring self pretty far: "If Terri Schiavo's desire is to die, then in fact, you're making her into a non-person by not following it." *Not* to kill her was to destroy her personhood because it was to disregard her will.

This dualism facilitates the denial of a right to life in cases where there is no reasoning, conscious self—as in abortion and the euthanasia of the "vegetative." As such, it is open to the same egalitarian objections mentioned earlier. But the party of death's dualism is also, as we saw in Chapter 7, untenable.

What pro-lifers opposed was an action—the removal of a feeding and hydration tube. This action didn't coincidentally result in death—the entire point was to cause death.

During Terri Schiavo's last days, we heard, perhaps, too much about God, and not enough about justice. As [the philosopher Immanuel] Kant said: "[S]uicide is not abominable because God has forbidden it; on the contrary, God has forbidden it because it is abominable." The commentariat seized on religious objections to killing Mrs. Schiavo, and were all too eager to engage in hyperbolic arguments about theocracy, rather than deal directly with the ethical issues involved in the Schiavo case.

The party of death even adopted a holier than thou stance, arguing that Christian conservatives were behaving faithlessly by striving to keep Mrs. Schiavo from attaining her eternal reward. If they really believed in the next life, went the argument, they would not have gone to such lengths to prolong this one. They were guilty of theological hypocrisy.

This was an extremely careless argument. To begin with, plenty of conservative Christians do not believe that anyone is *guaranteed* admission into Heaven. Worse, the argument wholly ignores the distinction between not prolonging someone's life and deliberately ending it. Nobody involved in the Schiavo case argued that heroic measures must always be taken to prolong the lives of dying patients (which, incidentally, Mrs. Schiavo was not until the tube was disconnected). Everyone, if asked, would have to concede that it could sometimes be permissible to take someone off life support, even when death was a predictable consequence of that action—if, for example, the patient preferred to die at home rather than in a treatment center. Nobody, with the possible exception of the DEA [Drug Enforcement Administration], opposes the use of pain medication to relieve suffering in every case where its use risks causing the patient's death. The claim that pro-lifers are "absolutists" on life cannot survive even cursory examination.

What pro-lifers opposed was an action—the removal of a feeding and hydration tube. This action didn't coincidentally result in death—*the entire point was to cause death*. The party of death pretended this distinction did not exist. If one followed this logic, churches should fund death squads to usher even more people into paradise (apparently, [cult leader] Jim Jones had the right idea).

It was in the middle of the Schiavo controversy that the Democratic party, already the party of abortion and of embryo-destructive research, started also to become the party of euthanasia. Many Democrats had voted to intervene in the case. But once the intervention turned out to be unpopular, they opted to pin the blame for it on the Republicans and, in particular, the "religious Right." There had never before been a national controversy about euthanasia that required the Democrats to plant their flag firmly in one camp.

Liberalism had once stood above all for the protection of the vulnerable. [Former U.S. vice president] Hubert Humphrey said that liberals looked to the well-being of "those who are in the dawn of life, the children; those who are in the twilight of life, the elderly; and those who are in the shadows of life, the sick, the needy and the handicapped." After a generation of supporting abortion, liberals are no longer so inclined. [Eric] Cohen concluded: "Instead of sympathizing with Terri Schiavo—a disabled woman, abandoned by her husband, seen by many as a burden on society—modern liberalism now sympathizes with Michael Schiavo, a healthy man seeking freedom from the burden of his disabled wife and self-fulfillment in the arms of another."

Howard Dean, the head of the Democratic party, vowed that Republicans would pay for trying to save Schiavo's life. Half a month after her death, he said, "We're going to use Terri Schiavo later on . . . This is going to be an issue in 2006, and it's going to be an issue in 2008." He may be overestimating the political potency of euthanasia as a cause. Those Americans who disapproved of Congress because they thought Republicans were politicizing a tragedy, or because they simply wanted it off their television screens, are unlikely to respond positively to Democratic attempts to pick the scab. In the months since Schiavo's death, no state has been moved to join Oregon in formally approving assisted suicide. (Schiavo, not being terminally ill, would not have been eligible for assisted suicide even in Oregon.)

Schiavo's death was surrounded by euphemisms, the need to resort to which also suggests a limit to the public's enthusiasm for euthanasia. Those who defended the withdrawal of the tube scrupulously avoided the words "starvation" and "dehydration." While the press was not allowed to witness her deteriorating condition, it was told that her "dying process" unfolded with soothing music in the background and a stuffed animal by her side.

But what the country tolerated was bad enough. If anyone on death row were ever starved to death, it would rightly be considered cruel and unusual punishment. Nobody would bother debating whether the federal government should step in.

People die every day, and people are killed every day. It's not every day, however, that most Americans support the deliberate killing of an innocent woman. Pro-lifers have always said that mercy killing is wrong, and also warned that once it started the mercy killers would cease to be fastidious about whether they were really following a patient's will. It's not just that the slope is slippery, but that we have already slid too far down it.

The Right-to-Die Movement Supports Death on Demand

Wesley J. Smith

About the author: *Wesley J. Smith is a senior fellow at the Discovery Institute and an attorney for the International Task Force on Euthanasia and Assisted Suicide.*

There is a pretense in contemporary assisted suicide advocacy that goes something like this: "Aid in dying" (as it is euphemistically called) is merely to be a safety valve, a last resort only available to imminently dying patients for whom nothing else can be done to alleviate suffering.

Meanwhile, in the real world, the founder of the Swiss suicide facilitating organization Dignitas is just about done with pretense. The *Sunday Times Magazine* (London) reported that Dignitas' founder, Ludwig Minelli, plans to create sort of a Starbucks for suicide: a chain of death centers "to end the lives of people with illnesses and mental conditions such as chronic depression."

Minelli believes that all suicidal people should be given information about the best way to kill themselves, and, according to the *Times* story, "if they choose to die, they should be helped to do it properly." Dignitas admits to having assisted the suicides of many people who were not terminally ill. As Minelli succinctly put it, "We never say no."

Core Belief of Euthanasia Movement

The story about Minelli illuminates a deep ideological belief within the euthanasia movement: that we own our bodies, and thus, determining the time, manner, and method of our own deaths, *for whatever reason*, is a basic human right.

That is certainly how one of the other superstars of the international euthanasia movement, the Australian physician Phillip Nitschke, sees it. Nitschke travels the world presenting how-to-commit-suicide clinics. Several years ago he was paid thousands of dollars by the Hemlock Society (now merged into the assisted suicide advocacy group Compassion and Choices) to create a suicide concoction made from common household ingredients (a formula he calls the "Peaceful Pill").

Like Minelli, Nitschke is straightforward about his goals. In a 2001 interview, *National Review Online* asked him who should qualify for the Peaceful Pill. He responded:

> *My personal position is that if we believe that there is a right to life, then we must accept that people have a right to dispose of that life whenever they want . . . So all people qualify, not just those with the training, knowledge, or resources to find out how to "give away" their life. And someone needs to provide this knowledge, training, or resource necessary to anyone who wants it, including the depressed, the elderly bereaved, [and] the troubled teen.*

Nitschke and Minelli's position has a large constituency among euthanasia believers. Indeed, over the years, the movement has left many telltale signs that assisted suicide is not intended ultimately to be restricted to the imminently dying.

Take the "Zurich Declaration," issued at the 1998 bi-annual convention of the World Federation of Right to Die Societies. (The WFRD is an umbrella group made up of 37 national euthanasia advocacy organizations, including Compassion and Choices and Hemlock founder Derek Humphry's Euthanasia Research and Guidance Organization, or ERGO.) It states:

> *We believe that we have a major responsibility for ensuring that it becomes legally possible for all competent adults, suffering severe and enduring distress, to receive medical help to die, if this is their persistent, voluntary and rational request. We note that such medical assistance is already permitted in The Netherlands, Switzerland and Oregon, USA.*

It should also be noted that one need not be dying or even sick to experience "severe and enduring distress."

Euthanasia Has Broad Support

Support for a broad and liberal access to suicide extends far beyond activists in the euthanasia movement. It has been embraced by some people in the mental health professions, where a concept known as "rational suicide" is being promoted in professional journals, books, and at symposia.

Typical of this genre is a 1998 article by James W. Werth published in the journal *Crisis*, with the ironic title, "Using Rational Suicide as an Intervention to Prevent Irrational Suicide." Werth urges that mental health professionals should not always save the lives of suicidal patients, but instead, should non-judgmentally facilitate the suicidal person's decision making process. If the professional agrees that the desire to die is rational, then the suicide should be permitted, or perhaps even assisted.

Respect for human freedom demands that society permit the suicides of competent persons—even when they are expressing an "unjustified desire to die."

To qualify for a rational suicide, the patient would have to demonstrate to the mental health professional that he has a "hopeless condition," which Werth defines as, "terminal illnesses, severe physical and/or psychological pain, physically or mentally debilitating and/or deteriorating conditions, or quality of life no longer acceptable to the individual." This is circular thinking. By definition, if one is suicidal, he has a quality of life that he believes is no longer acceptable.

Not surprisingly, assisted rational suicide is already permitted in the Netherlands where the Dutch Supreme Court approved a psychiatrist's facilitating the death of a distraught woman who wanted to die because her children were dead.

Similar suicide-friendly attitudes are often expressed among mainstream bioethicists—and not just by Princeton's Peter Singer. For example, the University of Utah's Margaret Pabst Battin suggests that "suicide can be rationally chosen," to "avoid pain and suffering in terminal illnesses," as a "self-sacrifice for altruistic reasons," or in cases of "suicides of honor and principle." Along these same lines, Julian Savulescu, an up-and-comer in the international bioethics community, argues that respect for human freedom demands that society permit the suicides of competent persons—even when they are expressing an "unjustified desire to die."

"Some freedoms are worth the cost of innocent life," Savulescu wrote in a chapter for the book *Assisted Suicide*. "The freedom to finish one's life when and how one chooses is, it seems to me, about as important as any freedom."

A Duty to Die

The right to receive assisted suicide for virtually any reason is especially popular among self-declared "free thinkers" and humanists. Thus, Tom Flynn, the editor of *Free Inquiry*, the house organ for the Council for Secular Humanism, wrote in the Spring 2003 issue, that the belief in human liberty must include an unfettered right to die. "While suicide has never been exactly popular, a new assault on our *right* to suicide is brewing. It's something secular humanists ought to resist." Why? Because Flynn (and other humanists) believe fervently that a right to suicide is a crucial element of human liberty:

> What's really in play here is the old dogma that individuals don't own their own lives. Physician-assisted suicide is but part of the issue. If we trust our fellow humans to choose their occupations, their significant others, their political persuasions, and their stances on religion, we should also defend their right to dispose of their most valuable possessions—their lives—even if disposing of life is precisely the choice they make.

There are even ongoing discussions in bioethics suggesting that some people might have an ethical *obligation* to commit suicide. Thus, a 1997 cover story in the prestigious bioethics journal the *Hastings Center Report*, philosopher John Hardwig argued that there is not only a right, but also a "duty to die":

A duty to die is more likely when continuing to live will impose significant burdens—emotional burdens, extensive caregiving, destruction of life plans, and yes, financial hardship—on your family and loved ones. This is the fundamental insight underlying a duty to die.

A duty to die becomes greater as you grow older. As we age, we will be giving up less by giving up our lives . . . To have reached the age of say, seventy-five or eighty years without being ready to die is itself a moral failing, the sign of a life out of touch with life's basic realities.

Bioethicist Battin has also supported the concept of an eventual duty to die for those living in rich countries, not just to spare burdening our loved ones but to promote world egalitarianism. Thus, she wrote in a book chapter called "Global Life Expectancies and the Duty to Die" that the time may come when we will have the moral obligation to "conserve health care resources by forgoing treatment or directly ending [our] life" toward promoting "health prospects and life expectancies" that are more equal around the globe.

Despite this thickening atmosphere of suicide permissiveness, most assisted suicide advocates in this country continue to insist that "all" they want is for the terminally ill to have access to hastened death.

For some, clearly, this is a mere political tactic. The ultimate goal is a much broader death license. Others may actually mean for the initial terminal illness limitation to be permanent, believing that "restricted" assisted suicide, once accepted widely, would not spread to ever widening swaths of acceptable killing (as it has in the Netherlands).

Which camp one decides best represents the overall euthanasia movement doesn't really matter. Once assisted suicide is accepted in law and culture, the premises of radical autonomy and allowing killing to alleviate human suffering would conjoin, unleashing the irresistible power of logic that would push us inexorably toward the humanist nirvana of death on demand.

The Lives of the Disabled Are Worth Living

Ron Amundson and Gayle Taira

About the authors*: Ron Amundson is professor of philosophy at the University of Hawaii at Hilo. Gayle Taira is a graduate student in philosophy at the University of Stirling, Scotland.*

The authors of this article have known each other for 20 years. We met as a professor of philosophy and an undergraduate philosophy major. The professor is still a professor. The student graduated, raised a family, and is now preparing for graduate school. We live in the same city and have remained in contact over the years. Neither of us is particularly interested in ethical or social philosophy. The professor does research in the history and philosophy of science, and the pending graduate student is interested in epistemology and metaphysics. We share one interest in social philosophy: the issue of physician-assisted suicide. We agreed on the issue in the early 1980s, and we agree on the issue today; but we have both changed our minds between those two times. . . .

Ron's Disability Story

I had polio in 1952 at the age of 6 years. The immediate effects were relatively minor, a weakened right leg and an oddly shaped foot. Like many polio survivors I was a "passer" for most of my life and didn't think of myself as disabled. Post-Polio Syndrome began to hit me in 1988. It affected me more than polio had, with weakening and chronic leg pain, and extreme exhaustion in the afternoons. In 1992 I began to use a wheelchair for mobility. This and other lifestyle changes help

Ron Amundson and Gayle Taira, "Our Lives and Ideologies: The Effect of Life Experience on the Perceived Morality of the Policy of Physician-Assisted Suicide," *Journal of Disability Policy Studies*, vol. 16, summer 2005. Copyright 2005 PRO-ED. Reprinted with permission.

me to manage the effects of Post-Polio Syndrome. I plan my day carefully, with regular rest periods and very efficient use of travel time. My home and work environment are modified, both for wheelchair accessibility and for the reclining posture that allows me to work without pain. These changes have allowed me to continue to work as a full-time academic. . . .

Our society used to worry about "the Race Problem" and "the Woman Problem." We now recognize that race and sex (the actual differences between races and between sexes) are not the cause of those problems. Destructive social attitudes are to blame. Racism and sexism are the names of the destructive attitudes. The disability-rights movement is based on identical reasoning. Bodily differences are not the causes of our problems, a destructive social prejudice is to blame; we call it ableism. Ableism is a doctrine that falsely treats impairments as inherently and naturally horrible and blames the impairments themselves for the problems experienced by the people who have them. Ableism is wrong. Disability is a social problem, not a medical problem. Impairments are not the problem; ableism is.

I began to notice that when assisted suicide advocates really wanted to scare their audience, they didn't use unremitting pain to do it. They used disability.

I report on this new concept of ideology not because I expect the reader to accept it. I know from experience that nondisabled people have a very hard time swallowing it (just like we all had a hard time recognizing our own racism and sexism). Nevertheless, when I replaced in my own mind the ideology of ableism with the ideology of the disability rights movement, it caused my conversion from an advocate to an opponent of physician-assisted suicide. That's why I am telling you about ableism.

Now I will explain how my rejection of ableism led to my rejection of physician-assisted suicide. It came from listening to the arguments made by assisted-suicide advocates in support of their positions. At the core of these arguments are a few classical cases of people with serious disabilities who wanted to commit suicide. The assisted-suicide advocates' use of these cases was blatantly ableist. They would describe the person's impairments in the most demeaning possible terms, and then ask "Wouldn't you want to die if you were in that position?" Their ableism was obvious from the fact that they took the impairments themselves as the true reasons for the death wish. From my (new) perspective it was obvious that these people wanted to die because of their social situation, not because of their impairments, in one case, a quadriplegic man was being forced to live in a filthy, restrictive, and geographically remote institution. He was refused the support he needed to live independently near his friends and family. Wouldn't you want to die if you were institutionalized against your will and taken away from your family? Of course. But the assisted suicide advocates blithely assumed that his quadriplegia alone, not his social circumstances, caused his despair. Because his quadriplegia could not be cured, he should have the "right to die." It never crossed their minds that his death wish would vanish if he were given the support he needed to live freely among his friends, as all human beings want to do.

I began to notice that when assisted suicide advocates really wanted to scare their audience, they didn't use unremitting pain to do it. They used disability. The need for help to go to the toilet was the big stick. Wouldn't you rather die than have someone else wipe your butt? It never seemed to cross these advocates' minds that thousands of people in the United States get help to wipe their butts every day. Many of them are my friends. The blatant disdain and scorn that the assisted suicide advocates showed for people with real disabilities disgusted me. I began to see the smug slogan "Death with Dignity" in a new light: It hid the assumption that dignity was forever out of the reach of people who were disabled; "Better Dead than Disabled."

I admit that this was a gut reaction, not a reasoned argument. Imagine listening to a charismatic speaker, and then suddenly realizing that he was a racist, and he had almost convinced you to join him in a lynching! After that first gut reaction of disgust toward the ableism of the assisted suicide advocates, I looked more carefully into the policy and its implications. I now have a reasoned basis for my opposition to assisted suicide, and I have not changed my mind.

Gayle's Disability Story

I graduated from college in 1987 with majors in history and philosophy. In 1992 I was teaching part time in the public school system and running my own home-based business tutoring and evaluating home-schooled students. These work arrangements were in place because I had a 9-year-old son and wanted to be home when he was home. That was the year my beliefs changed about assisted suicide. It happened literally by accident.

For many months I got up every morning hoping I would recognize the person facing me in the mirror.

In September 1992, I was in an automobile accident. A drunk driver crossed the center line and crashed into my car. My passenger was killed. I received serious brain injuries, along with numerous broken bones and contusions. At first my condition was very frightening to those who knew me. I could barely recognize my family and could not remember anyone's name. My ability to speak was extremely limited because of aphasia, and my physical injuries made gesturing impossible. I was diagnosed with traumatic brain injury (TBI), a condition from which I am still recovering and with which I am learning to deal.

For many months after the accident I had trouble with both short-term and long-term memory. I had difficulty speaking and doing arithmetic. I had to learn how to read again. I also had a visual—spatial difficulty: I did not know where my body was, so I often remained quite still, not even gesturing. In the early days I had little concept of time, and 2 minutes was the same as 3 hours to me. As a consequence, from the "outside," it often looked as if there was nothing going on "inside" of me.

TBI had drastically affected my access to my own memories. Ordinary sensory experiences, like tastes and sounds, seemed unfamiliar. I couldn't recognize my house or my clothing. I couldn't even recognize myself in a photograph. (I could sometimes guess, though. In family photos I picked out the blond one as "me," because my husband's family is Okinawan and I am not.) For many months I got up every morning hoping I would recognize the person facing me in the mirror. . . .

My approach to the physician-assisted suicide issue was completely changed by one single experience. It occurred right after my TBI and was the pivotal point in my interest in disability issues. In some sense it was an emotional reaction, but in another very real sense it was a philosophically reasoned change in view.

I was still in the hospital right after my automobile accident and sudden acquisition of TBI, going from one treatment center to another for innumerable tests. It is important to remember that TBI (and my inability to gesture) made it appear to some people that nothing was going on "inside" me. I found myself in a wheelchair in an elevator with two health care professionals. One woman was taking me to a set of medical tests. The other had joined us in the elevator. The first began to describe a car accident to the second person.

She described the injuries, and the cognitive difficulties that occur with TBI. The other woman said, "You know, I'd kill myself if that ever happened to me. I don't want to end up like that."

Like what? I wondered. Then I realized that they were talking about me, right then, right there. It was my accident she was describing, and the second woman would rather die than end up like me!

I suddenly realized (with a shock) that I had completely missed a crucial aspect of the physician-assisted suicide issue. I had incorrectly assumed that the individual making the choice would be free from coercion and would be making a choice based on his or her own interests, free from the forced perspective of others. I had assumed that the choices being offered were indeed legitimate choices. Talk about fatal assumptions! Sitting in the wheelchair in that elevator, I realized exactly how fatal that assumption is: The very people whose job it was to care for me believed that I would be better off dead, and I was powerless to argue against them.

Fortunately, I never felt forced to "choose" physician-assisted suicide. But if it were a legal option, and if my caregivers shared the opinion of the woman in the elevator, and if my ability to defend myself remained as low as it was at that time, how long would I have been able to hold out against the pressure to "freely choose" suicide?

Decisions are based on . . . ableist fear of disability, shame at needing help, dread of having someone else wipe one's butt.

My first reaction was that I really was not in favor of physician-assisted suicide. There was an entirely different view that I had neglected to consider, and I was annoyed with myself, because I had so completely missed the point—that although we can allow people to make their own choices about life issues, those choices are often constrained by the values and opinions of the caregivers. (Well now, which do I choose? Life with what my family and society views as unbearable pain, uselessness, boredom, and indignity? Or do I choose to kill myself, heroically sparing my family and society the time and effort to care for me?) My previous belief in the moral rightness of assisted suicide was based on the value of choice above all. Now I realized that the more important issue was whether a truly free choice was actually being offered.

My second reaction was annoyance with those health care workers: "What do you know about what I find enjoyable and pleasurable in my life?" And because I felt secure in my situation with my own family and caregivers, "What do I care about what you think?" But the fact is, when you are dependent on someone for basic daily care, you have to care what your caregivers think. If you are fortunate, like I was and am, you will have caregivers who let you choose what is meaningful to your own life and then help you pursue it. Many people are not so fortunate. What about those whose caregivers have different criteria about what makes life meaningful or worthwhile? What happens when someone is dependent on caregivers who tell them "I would kill myself if I were in your situation," and then is offered a legal choice between physician-assisted suicide and a life that is "a burden to others" and "completely devoid of meaning"? What kind of choice is that? . . .

Assisted Suicide Arguments Are Flawed

The typical arguments for assisted suicide are individualistic and personalized, based on the importance of individual choice over all else. They are flawed in two ways. First, they rely on the ableist prejudices of the audience: "Wouldn't you rather die than have someone else wipe your butt?" And second, the personalized form of the argument distracts the audience from recognizing that a social policy is being proposed.

That policy amounts to a social endorsement of the correctness of certain suicide decisions, and we all know what those decisions are based on. Oregon has informed us: Ableist fear of disability, shame at needing help, dread of having someone else wipe one's butt.

Liberals are not usually fooled by individualistic libertarian arguments. "Wouldn't you want the right to choose who lives in your neighborhood?" sounds good, until we recognize that the result is racial segregation. Assisted suicide sounds good when it's personalized (at least to worried, ableist listeners). But when it's you whose life is being judged as suicide-worthy, the social significance becomes obvious. When Gayle realized that the woman in the elevator was describing her life as not worth living, her conversion was instantaneous.

Here is one aspect of the social significance of a policy of legalized assisted suicide: The level of federal funding to support people with serious impairments. The United States has a shamefully low level of such support, and the present administration is intent on reducing it further. Social policies that even appear to endorse the claim that disabled lives are not worth living affect the public perception of the people who live those lives. If such lives are not worth living, why should we waste precious tax dollars on their support? If people with serious impairments are forced to live in degrading conditions, so be it. The ableist's ideology justifies this decision: The unhappiness of "those people" is caused by their impairments, not by the ableist's own lack of social conscience. This is the social harm caused by ableism and abetted by the assisted suicide movement.

Slippery Slope to Euthanasia

We (the authors) know all about the "safeguards" attached to assisted-suicide laws, such as the requirement for a terminal diagnosis. We do not trust them. For one thing, some of the leaders of the movement have made it clear that people with disabilities are the next step after people with terminal diagnoses. Second, the "safeguards" don't really make sense in themselves. If one were to consider death to be preferable to 6 months of disability, then surely one would consider death to be even more preferable to 50 years of disability. We oppose the premise that death is better than disability. The "safeguard" is just a quibble over the details.

We (the authors) have good news and bad news. The good news is that human beings are resilient. Young people often claim that they would rather die than get old. When they get old, they realize what fools they were when they were young. As oldsters, they are not obliged to commit suicide by their former lack of imagination about what makes life worth living. The same goes for acquiring a disability. It is possible for a person to create a perfectly delightful life under conditions that they never would have been wished for. Your previous, naïve lack of imagination ("I would rather die than . . .") is no barrier to the quality of your new life.

The bad news is that far too many people fail to recognize their own resilience. In their ableist pridefulness, many people are convinced that death is better than the loss of (what amounts to) their self-image—even in so trivial a matter as the self-image of a do-it-yourself toilet user. This tragic shortsightedness can result in suicides. Even worse, it can result in a social policy that implicitly endorses such grounds for suicide.

We oppose such a policy.

CHAPTER 4

How Can Suicide
Be Prevented?

Chapter Preface

More children and young adults die from suicide each year than from cancer, heart disease, AIDS, birth defects, stroke, and chronic lung disease combined. According to the United States Centers for Disease Control and Prevention (CDC), every year over 4,000 children and young adults commit suicide, making intentional self-harm the third overall cause of death between the ages of ten and twenty-four. Recently, the American College Health Association found that 61 percent of college students reported feeling hopeless, 45 percent said they felt so depressed they could barely function, and 9 percent felt suicidal.

One such college student was Garret Lee Smith. In 2003, the twenty-two-year-old, after a protracted battle with bipolar disorder and alcoholism, committed suicide. Popular and handsome, Garrett nevertheless fell into a trench of despondency while in college. He felt his life was pointless and wished that he could just go to sleep without waking up. Despite medical treatment, Garrett's life continued to spiral out of control. The day before his twenty-second birthday, he ingested a handful of sleeping pills and hanged himself in his college apartment closet. In his suicide note, he told his parents to "Put me in the ground, and forget about me."

Consumed by parental guilt, U.S. senator Gordon Smith (R-Oregon) championed the issue of youth mental illness and suicide. On October 21, 2004, one year after the death of the senator's son, President George W. Bush signed into the law the Garrett Lee Smith Memorial Act. The measure is the nation's first youth suicide prevention public act. The act authorized $82 million in grants over the next three years to help prevent suicide by young people. This act is important because it represents an initial step in establishing critical and needed support for mental and behavioral health services to students on college campuses. Moreover, the act acknowledges the considerable impact that mental and behavioral health problems have on a student's ability to succeed in college. A majority of the funds are directed to prevention strategies, which include screening, early intervention, assessment, treatment, management, and education with respect to mental and behavioral health problems that can lead to school failure, such as depression, substance abuse, and suicide attempts. These funds also are directed toward campus mental and behavior health services. They must be used for educational seminars; the operation of hotlines; preparation of informational materials; preparation of educational materials for families of students to increase awareness of potential mental and behavioral health issues; training programs for students and campus personnel to respond effectively to students with mental and behavioral health issues; or the creation of a networking infrastructure to link colleges and universities that do not have mental health services with health care providers trained to identify mental and behavioral health issues.

Youth Suicide Among Native Americans Can Be Reduced with More Federal Help

Cynthia Lindquist-Mala

About the author: *Cynthia Lindquist-Mala is president of Cankdeska-Cikana Community College, Spirit Lake Lakota, Fort Totten, North Dakota.*

Thank you, Senator, and thank you very much to the U.S. Senate Committee on Indian Affairs, Ms. Bumpas, Ms. Garland, and Senator Dorgan.

I do appreciate the opportunity to be here. I do not have prepared testimony and I will begin by saying [greeting in native tongue]. My friends, I am called Star Horse Woman, and I come from the Spirit Lake Nation. My professional role is president of Cankdeska-Cikana Community College, Spirit Lake Lakota, Fort Totten, ND.

I need to share with you, in sharing with you my Indian name, that I have a responsibility. I have come to understand in carrying my Indian name, my Dakota name, is to speak from my heart. I speak the truth as I understand it, as I have come to learn. I need to share with you that I have come up through the ranks professionally as my tribe's health director/planner in the early 1980's, a position I held for about 7 years. I have worked for the Indian Health Service at the regional and national level. I am an adjunct assistant professor of community health and rural health for the University of North Dakota School of Medicine and Health Sciences.

Cynthia Lindquist-Mala, "Youth Suicide Prevention: Hearing Before the Committee on Indian Affairs, United States Senate, Part 1," One Hundred Ninth Congress, 2005. Reproduced by permission.

Substance Abuse on the Reservation Is Unbelievable

Why I share that with you, and I am going to come back to my personal story, because I did grow up on the reservation, the Mission District, St. Michael, ND. When my parents went through a bitter divorce, I was a teenager. I went through what professional people called culture shock. I did not understand it at the time. But one of my reactions and responses to going through culture shock and not understanding my identity in being Dakota and Scandinavian, was that I took to alcohol and subsequently attempted suicide myself two or three times as a child.

Our children did not have that spark of life in their eyes. There was almost a sense of despair in young, young kids.

In my healing and learning journey, and especially my years as the tribe's health director/planner, the permeation of alcohol and substance abuse on the reservation was just unbelievable. So I made a conscious decision at that point in my life to set that aside. I couldn't be a hypocrite and be my tribe's health director/planner and have that lifestyle.

But alcohol and substance abuse affected everything in our lives and still does. I have been back home as the tribal college president for about 18 months. I have been truly blessed in my healing and learning journey and coming to terms with my identity and identifying as Dakota. But coming home after having national experience and getting to see Indian country from a national perspective, it is disheartening because of what is happening to our children.

I had a friend visit with me one time from England. We went to a couple of different reservations here in the Dakotas. After the end of the visit, we were just talking about the visit and getting her impressions. Her impressions were, she loved to be around the children, but at the same time, she was saddened, because our children did not have that spark of life in their eyes. There was almost a sense of despair in young, young kids. And I had never looked at it that way, especially having come off of being a tribal health director/planner and being so enmeshed in dealing with health and health issues. At that point in time, Spirit Lake Nation was dealing with four to five suicide attempts a week. We had one bachelor's level social worker.

To me, this suicide epidemic happening in Indian country is just a manifestation of all its history and reflects our community's historical oppression.

The program was a tribal health program. We retroceded it back to the Indian Health Service, and it is still with the Indian Health Service. We had contract psychologists and psychiatrists coming into the reservation. It is still that way. It hasn't changed, in all the years. That's what hurts, that's what breaks my heart.

I love being home, I love being a tribal college president. Because I am seeing optimism and hope in the student body at my college and the changes there.

Indian Suicide Is a Complex Issue

What I need to share with you all is that this is a very complex and serious issue, as you so eloquently stated in your opening, Senator [Byron L.] Dorgan. It is rooted in history. We can never forget that. It reflects broken treaties, broken promises. It is linked to what they call post-traumatic stress, that is so, for me, obvious now in Indian Country. It is linked to how and why we live the way we live. There are many policies passed with good intentions, but that did not work, that tried to change how we live. The essence of those policies was the dismantling of our families and the breakup of the structure of how our families lived and the way we lived.

To me, this suicide epidemic happening in Indian country is just a manifestation of all its history and reflects our community's historical oppression, the assimilationist policies meant to deal with Native people. Our people are wounded. Our people have wounded souls and wounded spirits.

The data from the deaths reflect communities and families in crisis. The healing has to begin by understanding, and understanding means different things to different people. We must understand and perpetuate a public understanding of Indian people in this country and its history. The dynamics of what is going on right now does in fact reflect this history. We need to create learning environments so non-Indian people understand better that history and the trauma that we are dealing with. We must create learning environments so our people have a better understanding also of this trauma and what we need to do to deal with it.

As these young people so eloquently stated, this issue of trust, this personal thing with trust, while most teenagers, it doesn't matter what culture or community you come from, most teenagers have this issue of trust. But for Native people and Native youth, it is especially compounded, because you have this historical trauma. We are fearful and we are mistrustful because of these broken promises, these broken histories.

At the same time, you look around, you look at the healing that is occurring, the wonderful resilience, survivability of the indigenous people of this country.

The Indian Health Service Needs More Funding

At the same time, you look around, you look at the healing that is occurring, the wonderful resilience, survivability of the indigenous people of this country, our compassion, our ability to forgive, our ability to continue to give and to give back. That is the essence of what is helping our people survive and looking forward until tomorrow, for all tomorrows, for the future.

So what can the U.S. Senate Committee on Indian Affairs do to address teen suicide in Indian country? Do what you are doing, Senator Dorgan. Have public forums, official and unofficial. We need to talk about it. We need to have mechanisms to do that in whatever way, whatever level, at different levels of Government, public, private, homes, churches, pow-wows, wherever. Gather that information and data, share it, disseminate it. Demand that the Federal Government, that Congress appropriate adequate resources for our health, our education of our people.

Off the top of my head, the Indian Health Service is funded at about 60, 65 percent of need. That gap is growing. It is not getting smaller. It is not diminishing. When I used to know these numbers, the mental health services and programs of the Indian Health Service were only funded at 20 to 25 percent of need. I don't think that's changed since I used to do Indian Health work. I think those numbers are probably comparable today. Likewise for education and education systems.

As the vice chairman of this committee, Senator, you could go forward and request that all the other Federal agencies open their doors for Indian programming, Indian services, Indian resources. Demand that based on this relationship, this unique relationship our people have with this country, that those promises be fulfilled. Assist in creating learning environments through education, health care programming. Have the faith-based organizations come to the table, be with us, and let's endeavor.

Better Training and Community Support

Create better training programs for our youth, for peer counselors, for our people to become mental health, behavioral health aides under the [Community Health Representatives program (CHR)] model that is so wonderful relative to being a liaison for health care and health care services. There needs to be setasides marked for tribal governments, tribal colleges, for each and every one of the Federal agencies to address this. It has to be a collaborative partnership. It cannot just be the Indian Health Service or [Substance Abuse and Mental Health Services Administration (SAMHSA)]. It has to be all of [Health and Human Services (HHS)], the Department of Education, the Department of Justice, Department of Commence, Department of the Interior, again, working together from a Federal, Congressional level down to the local level so it reaches our people.

We do have models. There are many wonderful models out there of community-based partnerships that are culturally appropriate, that are working. One I can just cite off the top of my head is Don Coyhis' Wellbriety program in the White Bison non-profit organization out of Colorado, grass-roots movement addressing alcohol and substance abuse issues. Really literally working in each individual district and community to bring national momentum toward addressing alcohol substance problems in Indian country.

Overall, there needs to be a sustained infusion of resources, both financial and human, to address this issue, and in a concerted and a partnership way. In closing, the word dakota, hopefully you understand or know it means friend or ally, it comes from a bigger word, wodakota, which means to be in harmony or balance. Indigenous culture has great beauty and understanding in this relationship we have with each other as human beings, the relationships we have with mother earth, and the things that we can bring forward relative to our knowledge of our healing powers, our resiliency that we do have here. It is working in many, many of our communities. It needs to be supported, it needs to be expanded.

We need to do what these young ladies asked us to do. We need to have activities for them, every day, 24/7. And a variety, youth centers, whatever. It is happening, it could happen more.

I thank you very much for having this today, Senator, and for your courage in taking the lead. [Phrase in native tongue.] We are all related.

Suicide Is Preventable if Treated as a Public Health Problem

Christopher Conte

About the author*: Christopher Conte is a staff correspondent for* Governing *magazine.*

In the mid-1990s, the United States Air Force was hit by a deadly epidemic: Every year between 1991 and 1996, about 60 airmen took their own lives, making suicide the second leading cause of death among the service's 350,000 members.

Eager to reduce the terrible toll, the service conducted "psychological autopsies" of the victims. These linked most of the suicides to problems airmen were having with the law, finances, intimate relationships, mental health, job performance and alcohol and drugs. The study also found most of the airmen were socially isolated and lacked the skills needed to cope with stress.

With these findings in hand, the service launched a counterattack. Top Air Force officials began urging airmen to seek assistance when they encountered personal difficulties, assuring them that doing so would not hurt their chances of promotion. The service also started training all its members in suicide risk-awareness and prevention, and it established "stress management" teams to help airmen and their families deal with potentially traumatic events.

These and other efforts worked. The suicide rate, which had been 14.1 per 100,000 active-duty service members from 1991 to 1996, fell to 9.1 per 100,000 from 1997 to 2002. Air Force officials attribute the improvement to the breadth of the program. "Suicide prevention," says one service manual, "is everyone's business."

Christopher Conte, "Dealing with Demons," *Governing*, vol. 17, August 2004. Reproduced by permission.

State Suicide Prevention Programs

The Air Force experience is getting a lot of attention these days in state capitols. At least 20 states have adopted suicide-prevention plans, most of them in the past few years, and many other states are working on the issue, too. Their efforts are driven by the belief that public health strategies, which involve looking for patterns that may point to the sources of disease and launching broad-based public information campaigns to encourage healthier living among the population at large, may hold the key to reducing suicide—just as they have been used to reduce heart attacks, strokes and lung cancer.

Suicide-prevention advocates sometimes seem to be acting more on faith than scientific proof.

Public health campaigns to discourage smoking, bad diet or unsafe sexual practices have become a familiar and remarkably successful part of American life, but the use of such strategies against a psychological disorder represents a significant new departure. If successful, it could usher in one of the most fundamental shifts in thinking about the role of state mental health programs in decades—one in which mental health agendas increasingly offer their services to the entire population rather than to the small group of people diagnosed as having severe mental illness.

"We have been missing opportunities to use public health promotion and prevention in the mental health sector," notes Alan Radke, who, as medical director for the adult mental health division of Hawaii's Department of Health, has been spearheading a broad review of prevention strategies for the National Association of State Mental Health Program Directors. "If we can demonstrate that the use of health promotion and prevention strategies works with suicide, from those learnings we can address any number of other conditions."

Suicide Is a Tough Problem to Solve

That's a big "if." The overall suicide rate has been stuck between 10 and 13 per 100,000 people annually for the past 50 years, and despite a handful of promising signs such as the Air Force program, there is no conclusive evidence that any strategy to reduce it will work. Indeed, suicide-prevention advocates sometimes seem to be acting more on faith than scientific proof. "When I started, I worried that this is too hard to fix and too big to understand," concedes Jerry Reed, executive director of the Suicide Prevention Action Network—USA, a lobby group that represents "suicide survivors," as family members of suicide victims call themselves. "But some times you have to act like a little bird, and hope when you leave the nest that you'll sprout wings before you hit the ground."

Although the prospects for success seem uncertain, advocates can offer some compelling reasons to tackle the problem. Suicide is the 11th leading cause of death in the United States, accounting for about 30,000 deaths a year. That's more than die from homicide (about 20,000 annually) or AIDS (14,000 a year). Moreover, researchers estimate that as many as 25 people attempt suicide for every one who actually kills himself. In 2002, some 250,000 people required medical treatment following suicide attempts, according to the Centers for Disease Control and Prevention. And surveys by the CDC show that 20 percent of teenagers have seriously considered killing themselves. (Much of the current push to combat suicide stems from a tripling of the rate among people aged 15 to 24 between 1950 and 1993, even though it has since leveled off.)

Suicide Is a Community Problem

Suicide survivors have played a central role in planting the idea that suicide is a community problem, rather than a private, individual matter. That is no small step, because suicide has long carried a stigma. "It took me a couple of years before

I could even talk about it," says Massachusetts state Senator Robert Antonioni, who lost a brother to suicide and has since persuaded the Massachusetts legislature to spend close to $1 million on suicide-prevention efforts over the past several years.

The important point, adds Kentucky state Senator Tom Buford, who steered a suicide-prevention bill through his state legislature this year partly in honor of his father who killed himself years ago, is that although "you feel you're living in sinful territory because somebody in your family committed suicide, after a while you see it's just an illness that needs to be treated."

At first blush, suicide seems different because it isn't a medical disease.

Because the majority of people who are suicidal go undiagnosed until it's too late to treat the illness, researchers say the only effective strategy may be to stress prevention in messages aimed at the entire population. "By reducing the risk for a lot of people, you get more bang for your buck than concentrating on the few who are at high risk," explains Kerry Knox, an assistant professor of preventive medicine at the University of Rochester.

The idea that broad strategies work more effectively than narrow ones against a hidden enemy is a fundamental tenet of public health. Epidemiologists liken society's approach to suicide today to its understanding of cardiovascular disease 30 years ago. Then, strokes, heart attacks and high blood pressure were treated largely on a case-by-case basis. The results were far from satisfactory because, as with suicide, these afflictions often went undetected until victims suffered crippling or fatal symptoms. But research in the 1970s and '80s showed that public information campaigns designed to promote low-cholesterol diets, exercise and screening for high blood pressure among the population at large were an effective way to prevent cardiovascular disease—even though many of the people who hear such warnings probably face little risk.

At first blush, suicide seems different because it isn't a medical disease. But the latest research suggests that it may not be so different. Like cardiovascular disease, it apparently results from both biological and environmental causes. People who commit suicide or attempt it have abnormalities in the prefrontal cortex area of their brains, which controls "inhibitory" functioning. Because of this biological condition, "they are less able to restrain themselves and more likely to have strong feelings," observes J. John Mann, chief of neuroscience at the New York State Psychiatric Institute. "When they get depressed, they get more depressed than most people." He concludes that suicide may be the product of "stress-diathesis"— that is, a confluence of "stressors" arising from the environment and a "diathesis," or predisposition for suicidal behavior.

Knox and Mann both serve on a suicide-prevention working group convened by the New York State Office of Mental Health (the Psychiatric Institute, considered one of the foremost research institutions in its field, is part of the state agency). Although they come from a public health and a neurobiological background, respectively, they agree that, as Mann puts it, "You need a combination of strategies to have an impact on the suicide rate." While he believes the day isn't far off when doctors will be able to detect people who have suicidal proclivities by reading their brain scans, the technology will be of little value unless people are willing to seek help for themselves or recognize when people they know need it. "You need to educate the public to understand there are such things as psychiatric illnesses, and that they can lead to suicide," he says. "That requires the involvement of government."

A Variety of Suicide-Prevention Efforts

Most states have started their suicide-prevention efforts with broad-based educational campaigns. This spring, for instance, New York State issued "SPEAK," which stands for Suicide Prevention Education Awareness Kits—packets of materials that explain the connections between depression and suicide and encourage help-seeking among teens, men, women and older people. Some states also offer advice to the news media on how to report on suicide. Guidelines adopted by Maine, for instance, seek to minimize the danger of "suicide contagion" by encouraging the press to refrain from describing how a person killed himself, glorifying a suicide and using such phrases as "successful suicide."

Some states have gone beyond educational programs to concentrate on strengthening the bonds that make for more supportive communities. In Alaska, where religious disillusionment and social breakdown are believed to lie behind high suicide rates among some native peoples, the state provides funds for village elders to teach children about their heritage. "This builds pride and relationships, so that if a kid gets in trouble later, he'll have somebody to turn to," explains Susan Soule, Alaska's program coordinator for suicide prevention and rural human services.

In the lower 48 [states], suicide-prevention programs seek to accomplish the same objective by training "gatekeepers"—clergy, doctors, teachers, social workers and others—who might come into contact with people who are suicidal. Paul Quinnett, president and chief executive of the QPR Institute in Spokane, Washington, believes that doctors, psychologists and social workers should be required to receive suicide-prevention training as a condition of being licensed. QPR, a deliberate take-off on the familiar emergency treatment CPR, stands for "Question, Persuade and Refer," a simple methodology for detecting people at risk of suicide and helping them get professional assistance.

North Dakota has provided its own version of suicide-prevention training to 28,000 people since 2000 on a budget of just $75,000 a year. The program seeks official gatekeepers as well as informal leaders—people who tend to pull communities together by force of personality rather than official position. "We go into schools and ask, 'Who is the person who makes things happen?'" says Mark Lomurray, the state's suicide-prevention project leader. "That's who we train." While Lomurray can't prove a causal connection, he notes that the number of suicide deaths in North Dakota has fallen by almost half since the program began.

We're reaching out to a much broader constituency than we ever did previously.

A Broad Constituency

It is too early to say if all the efforts surrounding suicide prevention will pay off, but if they do, state mental health programs may well need more money. "Right now, we do a good job identifying people who are suicidal, and we can refer them for services if there's a crisis," notes Cheryl DiCara, director of Maine's Youth Suicide Prevention Program. But for people who are troubled and haven't reached the crisis point, she says, "there's not a lot we can do."

Prevention advocates say that public health strategies may save money in the long run by reducing the need for acute care. But that implies new methods of serving people who don't need institutionalization. New York State offers some clues about where this more expansive orientation might lead. Traditionally, the Office of Mental Health has focused exclusively on helping people with severe mental disorders. After the September 2001 terrorist attacks, however, the department, with funding from the Federal Emergency Management Agency, began offering post-trauma counseling to the entire population of New York City and 10 surrounding counties. In two years, more than a million people availed themselves of these free counseling and educational services.

"We're reaching out to a much broader constituency than we ever did previously," notes Sharon Carpinello, New York's mental health commissioner. She expects the agency to become involved in a variety of new public health endeavors. In addition to suicide prevention, the agency is developing a disaster preparedness and "resiliency" campaign for the entire state and a separate campaign aimed at combating eating disorders in young women.

John Allen, who serves as the office's liaison with outside groups, says the new public health focus has brought enormous changes to his job. In the past, he mainly worked with a few small groups that represented patients in mental hospitals. But the post-9/11 project took him into the mainstream. One of his most important partnerships was with the New York State Thruway Authority, which helped the office distribute brochures to commuters. And the suicide-prevention program is bringing him into contact with major employers, local civic organizations and chambers of commerce.

As the department increasingly operates in a bigger arena, some prevention advocates hope it will start asserting itself on matters that previously have been beyond its ability to influence—including proposals to require insurance companies to offer the same coverage for mental illness treatments as they provide for medical care. The idea, of course, is very controversial because of the possible costs, but it's nothing compared with another issue that some prevention advocates have in their sights: gun control.

At the moment, there is no consensus even among suicide experts that stricter gun control would reduce the suicide rate over the long run. The best evidence is that making the leading instrument of suicide less available might have an impact for a while but that the improvement might dissipate over time as people switch to alternative methods to kill themselves. But the simple fact that the idea is even being discussed is a measure of how optimistic the mental health community is about the potential of public health strategies.

"I think we have to stay away from the more controversial strategies until society changes a little bit, but I don't feel totally hopeless," says Madelyn Gould, a research scientist at the New York State Psychiatric Institute who has participated in the state's suicide-prevention working group. "After all, who would have thought a couple of decades ago that anti-smoking campaigns would be so successful that today you can't even smoke anymore in bars in New York City?"

Classroom Discussion Can Help Identify Adolescents Who Are Suicidal

Douglas Fisher

About the author: *Douglas Fisher is a professor of language and literacy education at San Diego State University, California.*

What comes to mind when you think of the word adolescence? First dates? A driver's license? Hormones? If you are the teacher of one of the more than 500,000 young people who attempt suicide or the 5,000 who succeed in committing suicide each year, your view of adolescence may be a bit less jovial. Every two hours and 15 minutes, a person under the age of 25 completes a suicide. Since suicide is one of the leading causes of death for young people between the ages of 15 and 19, it's hard to imagine a high school teacher who hasn't been touched by this epidemic.

The issue is of such national significance that in September 2004, more than 350 members of the U.S. House of Representatives and the entire U.S. Senate voted to pass the Garrett Lee Smith Memorial Act, bipartisan legislation to reduce youth suicide. The bill authorized $82 million over three years for screening, assessment, and counseling.

While this seems like a great deal of money and it will certainly help educators address the problem of adolescent suicide, it will not work unless classroom teachers and building administrators serve as an early warning system. As teachers and administrators, we must be on the watch for the signs of adolescent suicide, and we must know how to respond when we come face to face with this daunting reality. Furthermore, we must confront this epidemic and provide space within schools for students to disclose their feelings to a trusting adult. Together with social services and healthcare providers, we can help reduce the toll of youth suicide.

Suicide Advance Warning Indications

According to the American Association of Suicidology (www.suicidology.org), approximately 80% of the people who attempt or succeed in committing suicide showed advance warning signs. Some of the signs of potential suicide in teens include:

- talking about committing suicide,

- having trouble eating or sleeping,

- experiencing drastic changes in behavior,

- withdrawing from friends and/or social activities,

- giving away prized possessions,

- having attempted suicide before,

- taking unnecessary risks,

- being preoccupied with death and dying,

- losing interest in personal appearance, and

- increasing use of alcohol or drugs.

Being gay, lesbian, bisexual, or transgendered or adjusting to feelings of attraction to members of the same sex may also present an increased suicide risk.

There are a number of issues for teachers and administrators to consider when such signs are present. Students disclose information about themselves in a number of ways, including in their conversations with peers and adults, in their writing, and in their behavior. How should we respond when we observe these early warning signs? Again, it is important to remember that teachers and administrators can serve as the early warning system that alerts the social and health services system to a youth in need. Most adolescent students do not know their school nurse, social worker, or psychologist very well. They often trust a teacher and reveal their problems to him or her first. As a result, despite a lack of training or support, the teacher becomes the broker of services for youths at risk of suicide.

Invite Discussion of Sensitive Issues

By the time they have reached adolescence, students know which topics are "off-limits" in school. While some students will discuss and write about things that matter in their lives, they are more likely to do so when such topics are seen as permissible. There are a number of ways educators can subtly inform students that they can discuss the issues that consume their thinking.

One common way to ensure that students know that they can discuss delicate issues with their teachers is to provide them access to books and information that explore these topics. These books can be in the school library or in a classroom library. In some cases, a teacher may give a specific book to a student to communicate that "you can talk with me about this." . . . Like much of the recently published adolescent fiction, books [those that address suicide] pull no punches and directly address the issues that our adolescents are struggling with.

As a case in point, Jerome (all names here are pseudonyms) was reading *The Burn Journals* [by Brent Runyon] and and said, "Man, I thought I had it bad. This guy hates life. I want to be alive and kickin' it." Colin was reading *Jay's Journal* [by Beatrice Sparks] when he said to his teacher, "Everyone at this school has thought out about it [suicide]. I get picked on 'cuz I'm so small and all. . . . I've thought about it. But Jay didn't know that death is a permanent solution to a temporary problem."

The teachers and administrators at Hoover High School in San Diego decided to address the issue more directly. During the opening weeks of school, the sustained silent reading period, which occurs for 20 minutes each day, was suspended. During this time, every teacher read aloud the book *Whirligig* [by Paul Fleischman]. A total of 2,300 students heard this book and discussed it with their teachers. In the first chapter, Brent goes to a party, is rejected, gets drunk, and attempts suicide by closing his eyes and taking his hands off the steering wheel. Of course, discussing this book schoolwide meant that the school had to be ready for students to discuss drinking, drinking and driving, and suicide. In many places, these would be forbidden topics. However, the Hoover faculty wanted students to know that these were real issues and that every student had a support system available.

Students who exhibit the warning signs of suicide need to have teachers adopt a professional approach.

Several days into the reading of *Whirligig*, Anna showed up in the classroom of one of her teachers with the book in her hand. She pointed to the line in which Brent attempts suicide and said, "This is me. I've tried this. I've tried it a lot." Fortunately, her teacher knew how to respond to the situation and convinced Anna to enroll herself in a support group for battered girls and a counseling program offered at the school.

Teaching Approaches

Certainly students' anxieties, concerns, and worries enter into the classroom discourse in a variety of ways and on a regular basis. As teachers, we can try to avoid these situations of disclosure by avoiding any personal conversations with students, either in writing or in discussions. Yet despite our efforts to steer clear of risky topics, they are inevitable and unavoidable. As Marti Singer noted, "Once we have read a paper, there is a contract between us and the person. . . . We need to respect the students' possible anxiety in telling the story at all . . . we need to ascertain what the writer needs and what our role is to be—advice-giver, classifier, info-giver, listener, facilitator, friend."

In 1995, Marilyn Valentino described the ways that teachers commonly respond to students' writing. While her focus was on writing, these behavioral patterns can be seen in any student/teacher discussions. Consider the following five approaches:

- The Ostrich Approach: ignore the comment altogether and say to yourself, "There is no problem. There is no problem."

- The Rush Limbaugh Approach: note the errors but ignore the content, as in "You missed an *i* in suicide."

- The Sally Jessy Rafael Approach: encourage more information and further disclosure without addressing the issue and providing guidance.

- The Dr. Quinn Approach: overreact, use "antiquated medicine to heal the patient," and misinterpret a need.

- The Professional Approach: recognize the pain while offering help and professional assistance and asking the person what he or she would like you to do.

Students who exhibit the warning signs of suicide need to have teachers adopt a professional approach. Thankfully, Anna's teacher knew this. As teachers and administrators, we have to become comfortable responding in this way to our students. In addition, students who have lost someone to suicide can benefit from writing about their thoughts, emotions, reactions, and experiences. In other words, writing can both allow us to identify students at risk and be therapeutic for students.

Teachers Must Confront Suicide Directly

Formal writing interventions can also be used to identify students at risk for suicide. One such initiative, an essay project of the American Psychiatric Association Alliance, is titled "When Not to Keep a Secret" and was developed in response to fears of school violence. The idea was to provide students with a formal opportunity to consider when keeping a secret was harmful. The instruction and associated writing enable students to reflect on their experiences in breaking a confidence and trusting an adult. While the program was developed to address school violence, approximately 90% of the papers submitted focus on suicide. . . .

The American Psychiatric Association Alliance has partnered with the Yellow Ribbon Campaign in its efforts to prevent suicide. The Yellow Ribbon Campaign provides guest speakers, training, online advice, an 800 hotline, request-for-help cards, and information across the country. Inviting guest speakers into schools is another way to help students understand that they are not alone in their experiences, thoughts, and needs and that there are adults around them who care.

While there are much happier topics I could have written about—from using graphic novels to engage struggling readers, to problem-based learning as a motivational tool, to establishing high expectations for all students—I believe that we educators must confront the issue of adolescent suicide directly. We must not follow the path of least resistance, the "ostrich approach." Nor should we blame the victim and his or her parents. Instead, we must provide students with an opportunity to seek and receive the help they need as they negotiate the trials, tribulations, and triumphs of adolescence.

The Suicide Rates of Sexual Minorities Need to Be Fully Researched

Ric Kasini Kadour

About the author: *Ric Kasini Kadour is a freelance writer and gay men's health advocate.*

Last June, a special issue of *Morbidity and Mortality Weekly Report (MMWR)* focused on suicide with the stated goal "to provide insights that might lead to successful prevention programs." The issue included articles on trends in suicide by young people, suicide attempts and physical fighting among high school students, school-associated suicides, suicide among Hispanics, and suicidal behavior in China. *MMWR* is a publication of the Centers for Disease Control and Prevention, and its purpose is to alert public health officials about emerging trends, issues, and outbreaks of disease. On occasion it dedicates an issue to a single theme in order to draw attention to important topics.

Suicide is the eleventh highest cause of death in the United States, third among ten-to-24-year olds, and in 2002 was the cause of over 124,000 visits to emergency rooms in the U.S. The prevention of suicide is a national priority, and objectives to track and ultimately reduce suicide are included in *Healthy People 2010*, the nation's health promotion plan. Countless studies over the past ten years document the fact that gay youth are at increased risk for attempting suicide. Studies have appeared in publications such as the *Archives of General Psychiatry, International Journal of Eating Disorders, Pediatrics, Archives of Pediatrics and Adolescent Medicine, Journal of Gay and Lesbian Social Services, Journal of Pediatrics, Social Work, Ameri-*

Ric Kasini Kadour, "The Power of Data, the Price of Exclusion," *The Gay and Lesbian Review*, vol. 12, January–February 2005. Copyright 2005 Gay & Lesbian Review, Inc. Reproduced by permission.

can Journal of Public Health, and *Journal of Adolescent Research,* and in reports published by the states of Massachusetts, Oregon, Vermont, and Washington. Of all the issues that affect gay youth there is no other issue on which there's so much consensus as on gay youths' risk of suicide.

And yet, despite this robust finding, no mention of sexuality appears in the 28-page *Morbidity and Mortality Weekly Report* for June 2004. In July 2004, a similarly glaring omission appeared in an *MMWR* report on violence among high school students. A product of the federal government, the *MMWR* is subject to the same political pressures as other parts of the Department of Health and Human Services. So it should come as no surprise that the editors of the *MMWR* would shy away from open communication about sexuality. The omissions, however, raise questions about the ability of the federal government to succeed in securing the health and well-being of its citizens.

The United States Is Unique in Its Approach to Health

Unlike most other countries, the United States takes a disease-specific rather than a population-specific approach to health. That means that rather than examine a group of people to determine what health issues affect them, public health officials in the U.S. examine a disease and ask which groups are affected by it. Instead of a department of sexual minority health, there is an AIDS program, a division of tobacco control, and so on. The resulting system is one in which the needs of minorities are hidden in half a dozen programs scattered across an ocean of public health bureaucracy.

Imagine for a moment living in an America without a public health infrastructure. No one tracks disease or monitors the safety of food and drinking water. Emerging epidemics fester unnoticed until they ultimately cycle out of the surviving population, faded into memory and legend. Habits may die hard, but without health promotion they don't die at all. People continue to smoke, eat poorly, not exercise, and have sex without understanding the risks to their well-being and how to minimize those risks. Life expectancy would be lower than it currently is; infant mortality would be higher; and the overall quality of life would be lower than what Americans now enjoy.

At a time when government is being strangled and bled, it's important to remind ourselves that government plays a vital role in maintaining our ability to thrive: to move around, to stay healthy, to be safe. When sexual minorities are not included in government definitions, they inevitably miss out on some of the benefits of public health. As a result, health indicators (such as smoking rates) are often much worse for sexual minorities than for the general population.

When sexual minorities are not included in government definitions, they inevitably miss out on some of the benefits of public health.

Data Are the Key to Public Health Care

Data are a cornerstone of any public health system, and the lack of data on sexual minorities correlates with the failure of public health to address this group's needs. Information generated by the scientific community informs policy set by legislators and regulatory agencies. Citizens groups also play a critical role: be it a working committee at the National Institutes of Health or an advisory body of a local health department, citizens across America create policy every day. Most of the time, that policy is rooted in science: peer-reviewed, published research that's used to determine which problems need to be addressed and how; and more importantly, how money is to be spent. High-quality scientific research is vital to our ability to address problems.

"One of the greatest threats to the health of lesbian, gay, and bisexual (LGB) Americans is the lack of scientific information about their health," asserted Randall Sell in the June 2001 issue of the *American Journal of Public Health*. Sell is a Columbia University professor who was contracted by the U.S. Department of Health and Human Services to review sexual orientation data collection practices at the department. "Without adequate information on the health of LGB Americans, measurable advances in civil rights and basic health will be difficult to achieve."

Without data, it's difficult to establish meaningful policy. For example, if you want to reduce the rate of tobacco use in the gay population, you first have to know what proportion uses tobacco, and also why they do so. And after you've launched an effort to tackle this problem, you'll need to find out whether or not the policy or program is working, and you'll need to look at the data over a period of time to determine its impact.

When left out of research such as this, sexual minorities become invisible, not just in the annals of science, but at the policy table as well.

Researchers already gather this sort of information for the general population and for racial and ethnic minorities. What they don't do is ask questions that allow the data to be analyzed specifically for sexual minorities. And why not? Researchers often make the claim that it's especially difficult to gather information on sexual minorities. First, there is the conundrum of whether to ask about identity ("Are you gay?") or behavior ("Who do you have sex with?"). Then there's the issue of honesty: since information is gathered over the telephone or in person, members of sexual minorities may be reluctant to reveal themselves when asked.

Sexual Minorities Are Invisible

A methodology for collecting data on sexual minorities has been around since the early 1990's. Various surveys approach the question from diverse angles to ascertain the attraction, behavior, and/or identity of the respondents. Data collection systems such as the U.S. Census, the HIV/AIDS Surveillance System, and the Youth Risk Behavior Surveillance System have incorporated some aspects of data-gathering on sexual orientation, identity, and attraction. Having said that, there is as much consensus on how to collect data on sexual orientation as there is on collecting data on racial and ethnic status, which isn't much. This is where homophobia is different from racism. The prospect of asking subjects whether or not they are gay disturbs many public health officials and researchers. Heterosexuals may be offended by the question. Sexual minorities often distrust how the information will be used. The problem of how to collect data is often used as an excuse for not collecting data at all.

Still, researchers routinely ask subjects about matters that would otherwise be considered private. Take, for example, a study from the *Journal of Interpersonal Violence* (January 2004) entitled "Sexual Deviance Among Male College Students." Researchers at Southeast Missouri State University wanted to determine whether group affiliation or prior deviant acts was a better indicator of sexual deviance among male college students. They surveyed male athletes and fraternity members about whether or not they had, in the past, engaged in generic deviance (driving recklessly, stealing, drug use, etc.) and coercive sexual behavior (a range of non-consensual contact such as kissing, hand-holding, sexual touching, intercourse). The use of gender neutral language in the article's conclusion is curious given that the subjects of the study are male and the questions that made up the coercive sexuality scale were entirely heterosexual: "Kissed a female against her will?" or "Ignored a female's protests before or during sex?" We know from other research that men who rape other men tend to be heterosexual. So why these researchers couldn't find a gender-neutral way to ask this question is not at all clear.

When left out of research such as this, sexual minorities become invisible, not just in the annals of science, but at the policy table as well. While heterosexual sexual assault prevention programs can use this study to inform funding applications, establish policy, and justify programs, those wanting to prevent same-sex sexual assault cannot. Prior deviance may predict same-sex sexual deviance, as this study suggests it predicts heterosexual sexual deviance, but in the end we just don't know.

Heterosexism Is Widespread in Research

How research is published is often a complicated process. In theory, disciplines establish standards while editorial boards and peer-reviewers maintain those standards through rigorous examination of research before it is published. Few journals publish standards, but professional associations who are often also publishers of research do have codes of ethics.

The pervasiveness of racism and heterosexism should not come as a surprise.

The American Psychological Association's (APA) code of ethics states "scientific or professional knowledge in the discipline of psychology establishes that an understanding of factors associated with age, gender, gender identity, race, ethnicity, culture, national origin, religion, sexual orientation, disability, language, or socioeconomic status is essential for effective implementation of their services or research." But the APA's own body of research reveals a pattern in which demographic factors are either the subject of study (i.e., how racial and sexual minorities think and act) or wholly absent (i.e., how generic people in general think).

An article published in January 2004 examined the relationship between memory and stigma in older adults. "Explicit and Implicit Stereotype Activation Effects of Memory," published in *Psychology and Aging*, one of the APA's many journals, compared responses to standardized memory tests to determine whether or not positive and negative aging stereotypes had an effect on memory in older adults. The study, which comes out of a wealth of research on the effects of social context on aging, fails to take minority status into account, instead making the assumption that older adults don't differ in important ways because of their demographic profile. And yet, racial and sexual minorities have a very different relationship to social context than do their straight white peers. The lack of differentiation is a glaring flaw of the study, and the reductionism employed by the researchers invalidates racial and sexual minorities and seems to violate, if not the letter, then at least the spirit of the APA's code of ethics.

The pervasiveness of racism and heterosexism should not come as a surprise. The sad truth is that the articles mentioned here are representative of most research produced by the scientific community. Whether researchers are motivated by ignorance, indifference, or purposeful exclusion is not clear; one suspects a combination of all three. Change will only come when the editorial boards of those journals that publish such research require scholarship to include accurate demographic data pertinent to sexual minorities. What is needed are more sexual minorities serving as peer-reviewers and working within organizations to implement standards that address these issues.

Beyond these specific actions, sexual minorities need to demand greater inclusion in scientific research and data gathering. Research isn't only published in peer-reviewed journals. Newspapers and television news programs often report on research findings. The more people ask why sexual minorities are not being included, the more likely it is that they'll be included in future research.

Teenscreen Is an Effective Teen Suicide Prevention Program

Arline Kaplan

About the author: *Arline Kaplan is senior contributing editor for* Psychiatric Times *and senior contributing editor to* Geriatric Times.

Aware that mental illness generally begins early in life and that four teen-agers commit suicide every day, several organizations and agencies are stepping up efforts to expand voluntary mental health screening and suicide prevention initiatives for youth—but they are doing so in the face of stigma and vocal opposition.

Child psychiatrist Kenneth Duckworth, MD, speaking on behalf of the Campaign for Mental Health Reform, a national partnership of organizations representing the mentally ill, their families, service providers and many others, said at a Congressional briefing last year, "We strongly believe that voluntary mental health screen with parental consent and involvement can have a huge benefit for youth at risk of mental and emotional disorders".

Yet, these efforts are being met with resistance by opponents who claim screening will lead to the "labeling" and "drugging" of children and interference with parental rights.

Mental Illness Can Be Detected at an Early Age

Well informed about the controversies, child psychiatrist Steven Adelsheim, MD, former director of and now consultant to New Mexico's school mental health program, told *Psychiat-*

ric Times that voluntary mental health screening programs are critical for safety and suicide prevention.

Suicide among teen-agers is a national problem, he pointed out. It is the third leading cause of death among teen-agers. In 2002 (the latest year for which data is available), 1,531 children 15 to 19 years of age, and 260 between 10 and 14 years of age committed suicide. New Mexico, Adelsheim said, has the fifth highest rate of teen suicide in the country. Last year, the New Mexico Department of Health was among 14 state-sponsored youth suicide prevention and early interventions selected to receive an estimated $400,000 each in federal funding from the Substance Abuse and Mental Health Services Administration (SAMHSA). The grants were made possible by the Garrett Lee Smith Memorial Act.

New Mexico's challenge with regard to youth suicide is outlined in the 2003 New Mexico Youth Risk and Resiliency Survey, which involved 103 of 191 high schools in the state and 11% of the high school students. Researchers found that nearly 31.9% felt so sad and hopeless almost every day for two or more weeks in a row that they stopped doing their usual activities; 20.7% seriously considered attempting suicide, 14.4% attempted suicide one or more times in 2003, and 7.5% indicated that their attempt required medical attention by a doctor or nurse. For comparison, 16.9% of a national sample of 15,000 high school students surveyed the same year reported they have seriously considered attempting suicide, 8.5% have actually attempted it one or more times during a year and 2.9% needed medical attention.

Since many mental health disorders, such as anxiety and impulsive control disorders, begin in childhood or adolescence, it is wise to identify them early to avoid treatment delays, said Adelsheim, also associate professor of psychiatry, family/community medicine and pediatrics at the University of New Mexico Health Sciences Center.

He pointed to research published last year in *Archives of General Psychiatry* that indicated half of the individuals who develop a mental health disorder in their lifetimes exhibit symptoms before age 14 and three-quarters by age 24 years. What's more, those same reports revealed a substantial delay in the time from illness onset to the time people get treated (e.g., delays of six to eight years for mood disorders and nine to 23 years for anxiety disorders).

A vocal opponent of the early detection concept ... [argues] that it negates parental rights, encourages overmedication of children and is unsupported by evidence that it decreases suicide attempts.

"So it seems to me that being able to identify kids at risk early and then linking them early to services will decrease the chronicity of illness and will decrease the seriousness of other risk factors that might develop, such as violence, suicide, teen pregnancy and/or substance abuse problems," Adelsheim said. "When we are looking at depression and other mental health conditions, there is real value in identifying these problems early, getting kids services and getting them back on track in school."

Mental health problems that go undetected and untreated frequently persist, leading to educational ramifications as well, he added. A child who is very depressed or has other mental health problems that go untreated isn't going to learn or become a productive citizen.

TeenScreen Opponents

A vocal opponent of the early detection concept is Rep. Ron Paul (R-Texas), a physician, who in 2004 and 2005 introduced legislation to prohibit the use of federal funds for a "universal or mandatory mental health screening program," arguing that it negates parental rights, encourages overmedication of children and is unsupported by evidence that it decreases suicide attempts. Paul's legislation (which did not pass) was backed by some anti-psychiatry and conservative political organizations, including Concerned Women for America, Gun Owners of America and the Eagle Forum. Paul's legislation particularly sought to prevent grants to states to implement recommendations of the President's New Freedom Commission on Mental Health, [which were released in July 2003].

Additionally, in several states across the United States, legislation has been introduced that prohibits mental health screening of children in schools, prohibits school personnel from recommending psychotropic drugs for children and limits the ability of school personnel to make recommendations or even have dialog with parents about behavioral health diagnoses, according to the National Mental Health Association (2005). States with such legislation have included: Alaska, Florida, Georgia, New Mexico, New Hampshire, New York, Pennsylvania, Tennessee, Utah and Vermont. In both Utah and Florida, the legislation was passed by the legislature but vetoed by the governors.

Seven of 41 states that currently have suicide prevention plans specifically mention TeenScreen by name.

Much of the controversy over mental health screening stems from an endorsement of the practice by the President's New Freedom Commission on Mental Health. While the commission has been accused of calling for mandatory screening without parental consent, Michael F. Hogan, PhD, director of the Ohio Department of Mental Health and chairman of the commission, in a 2004 letter to the *Washington Times*, said:

The commission did not call for mandatory universal mental-health screening for all children. I am at a loss to explain why this misrepresentation persists, since it is at odds with the plain language of our report to the president. . . .

[T]he commission proposed broad screening only in settings where many children are known to have untreated behavioral problems. Beyond this, the commission promoted programs that provide voluntary screening only with parental consent.

A SAMHSA backgrounder recently pointed out that the Administration does not support mandatory screening nor screening of children without parental consent.

TeenScreen Is Widely Used

One of the model screening programs identified in the New Freedom report was TeenScreen, created by Columbia University in New York City, under the leadership of David Shaffer, MD, director of the Division of Child and Adolescent Psychiatry at Columbia University. It has become the most widely used mental health screening program for teen-agers, with more than 450 active screening sites in 43 states. According to data from the Suicide Prevention Resource Center, seven of 41 states that currently have suicide prevention plans specifically mention TeenScreen by name: New York, Florida, Iowa, Nebraska, New Mexico, Oregon and Vermont. Additionally, Teen-Screen has trained individuals to conduct screenings in Panama, South Korea, Colombia and Australia.

"For 2005, based on the projections we get back from our sites, we think approximately 122,000 kids [in the United States] were offered the screening, and about 55,000 actually did the screening," Leslie McGuire, MSW, director of Columbia University's TeenScreen Program, said in an interview with *Psychiatric Times*. Since the program's initiation in 1999, McGuire estimated that 100,000 teen-agers have been screened. About 16% to 17% of those screened received a referral for a complete mental health evaluation.

"Our ultimate goal is to make mental health checkups available to all American teens," said McGuire. "I don't mean that every kid should be screened, but that this should be something that is available for our kids just like other health screenings are."

Laurie Flynn, executive director of the Carmel Hill Center for Early Diagnosis and Treatment, which oversees the Teen-Screen Program, and executive director of TeenScreen, likened TeenScreen to an early warning system. "We are very eager," she said, "to find those youngsters who may be at risk for serious psychiatric disorders, to identify those youngsters and alert their families so they can make the best decisions about further assessment and appropriate treatment."

The issue of youth suicide prevention is personal to Flynn; her daughter made a suicide attempt during her senior year of high school.

"Certainly having the experience as a parent of dealing with a youngster, who suddenly became depressed and suicidal, was stunning and certainly galvanizing. I never experienced anything as terrifying and for which I felt quite as unprepared," she told *Psychiatric Times*, adding that she wished a program like TeenScreen had been in place when her daughter's illness struck.

The TeenScreen program uses scientifically validated questionnaires to help identify teen-agers at risk. Currently, sites have the option of picking between three different screens:

1. The Columbia Health Screen, a 14-item self-completion, paper-and-pencil questionnaire used to identify risk factors of suicide;
2. The Columbia Depression Scale, a 22-item, self-completion, paper-and-pencil questionnaire that includes questions about the symptoms of depression and suicide ideation and attempts; and
3. The Diagnostic Predictive Scales, a 52-item, computerized interview that screens for social phobia, panic disorder, generalized anxiety disorder, major depression, alcohol and drug abuse, and suicidality.

All of the screening instruments, which take between eight and 10 minutes to complete, were developed and tested at Columbia University.

"We know those screens and the research base for those screens well, and we are able to provide specific training in how to use them, and how to interpret the results," Flynn said.

"Typically, we bring the folks to New York, and they will spend one full day in a training session at Columbia. Sometimes, we go out to a site, if we are training a lot of people at once," Flynn added. Recently, TeenScreen hosted its first conference. More than 200 attendees received updates on research and were able to share information on techniques that are effective in screening and suicide prevention.

Currently, the TeenScreen Program offers its screening instruments, materials, software, training and consultation services at no cost.

"We have never had any sponsorship other than private philanthropy here at Columbia, which has been useful in the wake of these erroneous allegations that we are somehow promoting one or another kind of treatment. . . . Because, in fact, we never have, we don't and that's not our role," Flynn said.

There are several ways that communities can make mental health screening available to youngsters and their families, at minimal cost, according to Flynn.

Sometimes, there is a school health clinic, and the screening becomes part of the health checkup process.

Sometimes, the staff of a community mental health center will come into a school or community-site and provide the screening to youngsters. Sometimes, a local mental health association will have a contract with the school district to provide the service.

"We've worked with the State Department of Education in Iowa, Office of Drug Control in Florida, with a student assistance program in the schools in Pennsylvania . . . wherever there is energy and interest," Flynn added.

TeenScreens Are Voluntary and Require Parental Consent

Flynn emphasized that the screenings are voluntary and require parental consent and involvement.

"Nobody cares more about family privacy than I do, and nobody respects more of the role of families in mental health services and decision making than I do," said Flynn who served as executive director of the National Alliance for the Mentally Ill for 16 years.

She explained that both parental consent and participant assent is required before a youth can participant in the screening process.

"We have given our sites standard letters and forms and recommended models they can use and adapt. So, I think we have been an exemplary program in the use of consent," she said.

"We are about identifying potential for risks, alerting the parents, and then parents can choose what to do next. Parents need to be informed about their options, but we didn't want to look like we were coming with 'the solution,'" Flynn said.

McGuire explained the general process once a teen-ager screens positive on one of the TeenScreen instruments. The teen-ager immediately will have a clinical interview with a mental health professional to determine if they need a complete evaluation. If an evaluation is determined necessary, a TeenScreen case manager meets with the teen-ager and contacts the parents to inform them of the screening results and the clinician's recommendations. The issues are explained in detail.

"It is not enough to call up and say, 'We have screened "Leslie", and we think she's got depression and needs to be evaluated for that, good luck,'" said McGuire. "You need to explain what depression is, how it can impact the child and his or her functioning, what happens when depression is not treated and then offer the family assistance in finding a place where the child can be evaluated."

Families without insurance are given assistance in getting help through public programs.

TeenScreen Works in New Mexico

In New Mexico, Adelsheim said that currently 14 different school districts around the state are using some version of TeenScreen at their school-based health centers. He expects that number to grow, since additional state funding is enabling the number of school-based health centers to grow from 34 to 68.

"We have been looking at the issue of how we are going to build more TeenScreen models across the school-based health centers throughout the state," said Adelsheim, who is now a consultant for New Mexico's Behavioral Health Purchasing Collaborative.

In one survey of parents whose children were identified through TeenScreen, 72% reported that their child was doing very well or significantly improved.

Work with TeenScreen in New Mexico began in 2001 through a collaborative relationship with the New Mexico Department of Health's Office of School Health and the University of New Mexico's Department of Psychiatry. As a pilot test, the TeenScreen Program began at five school-based health centers, one of which was in the Native American community of Acoma-Laguna. The pilot led to the stationing of a Teen-Screen Program Western Regional Coordinator in Albuquerque, integration of the TeenScreen Program into several Robert Wood Johnson-funded research grants and the adoption of screening by several frontier schools.

In the state, Adelsheim explained, TeenScreen serves as a secondary screening tool after students are first identified as being at risk on a statewide initial information screen administered at school-based health centers.

"We really only train sites on the use of TeenScreen where we have had an adequate number of mental health providers on site to be available to provide services to the youth who ended up with a positive screen. So we haven't used it really in a broad-brush, universal approach," he said.

To assist school-based health centers in rural areas, Adelsheim said child psychiatrists from the University of New Mexico are visiting some areas one or two days a month, working with the schools and seeing some of the kids identified as being at risk for mental health problems or suicide. Also, a Telehealth project launched this year is enabling child psychiatrist consultants to provide backup consultations.

Nationally, questions have arisen as to the efficacy of voluntary mental health screenings for youth. A follow-up study of teens referred to treatment following screens found that the majority of youth identified as at risk got help. Parents reported that 47% of teens referred to a mental health professional received help within the first three months of the screening and that number grew over time. Six months after screening almost 60% had received assistance. In one survey of parents whose children were identified through TeenScreen, 72% reported that their child was doing very well or significantly improved after participating in the screening program and seeing a mental health professional. . . .

On a personal level, Flynn is aware of teen-agers identified through TeenScreen who have gotten help and are doing well. She described a young African-American female who, at age 15, was very depressed and on the verge of dropping out of high school. The teen-ager was identified as being at risk through TeenScreen and received treatment. Now, she has completed high school and is midway through college.

After connecting to treatment, she was asked why she didn't tell someone she was in trouble and needed help. Flynn said her answer was very poignant and one she hears all the time: "Nobody ever asked me."

Collegiate Suicide Prevention Programs May Increase the Number of Suicides

Thomas Szasz

About the author: *Thomas Szasz is a professor of psychiatry emeritus at State University of New York (SUNY) Upstate Medical University in Syracuse.*

N*ulla poena sine lege* (No penalty without law). The rule that a person cannot be penalized for doing something that is not prohibited by law has long been viewed as a fundamental principle of free societies.

American criminal law does not prohibit suicide. De jure [according to the law], it is legal to kill yourself. De facto [in reality], if you do so, others may be punished, and punished harshly. Our legal system often holds innocent individuals and institutions responsible for the self-murder (as it used to be called) of persons whose suicides they are supposed to prevent. This perversion of the law is destroying the moral and legal fabric of our society.

For centuries, suicide was a grave sin and a capital offense. The suicide as well as his family were harshly punished by both ecclesiastical and secular-legal sanctions. Today, the successful suicide is exonerated of "self-murder" with an automatic posthumous diagnosis of mental illness, and his family may be enriched by imputing guilt for his "wrongful death" to innocent third parties. The unsuccessful suicide ("suicide attempter") is also automatically considered mentally ill; he is stigmatized as insane, deprived of liberty by psychiatric incarceration, and subjected to involuntary psychiatric "treatment."

Thomas Szasz, "College Suicide: Caveat Vendor," *The Freeman*, vol. 55, May 2005. Copyright 2005 Foundation for Economic Education, Incorporated. www.fee.org. All rights reserved. Reproduced by permission.

Pro forma [as a formality] suicide has been decriminal-ized. De facto, suicide has been "criminalized" by turning the non-prevention of self-murder into a tort (civil law offense). Contemporary mores and civil law define colleges, for ex-ample, as standing in loco parentis [in place of parents] to college students; the students are cast in the role of standing in loco infantis to college personnel; and the substitute "par-ents" have the duty to prevent the child-students' suicides and suicide attempts.

College Suicide Prevention Programs Are a Fraud

A report in the October 15, 2004 issue of the *Wall Street Jour-nal* was entitled: "Some colleges try zero-tolerance toward sui-cide attempts." Normally, we use the term "zero-tolerance" in connection with illegal acts, such as trafficking in prohibited drugs. Here the *Journal* casually uses it in connection with acts that are not only legal but usually are not "suicide at-tempts" at all.

College suicide prevention programs have nothing to do with preventing suicide: they are charades that give the illusion that the "responsible" parties are behaving re-sponsibly.

We learn that at the University of Illinois, for example, the "frontline . . . of the [suicide prevention] program consists of about 1,000 people—from dorm staff to deans—who are re-quired to file a formal suicide report any time they hear about or witness a threat or attempt." What is there to prevent Alice from denouncing Elizabeth, claiming that she has talked to her about suicide? Of course, Alice is considered to be pro-tecting Elizabeth, not denouncing her. And Elizabeth is being given an "option," she is not punished.

A female student at the University picks up a power cord from a light fixture and wraps it around her neck in front of her boyfriend. He calls 911. University officials tell the student: "Meet with a mental health counselor for four sessions or don't bother coming back to school the following semester. . . . [T]he university has a zero-tolerance rule with suicidal behavior."

The university is a very old institution. Through centuries—when the pupils were much younger than they are now—the student's suicide was not the business of fellow students, teachers, or university administrators. Why is it now? Because formerly the student who killed himself sinned. Now we say he was sick. And we don't punish illness.

However, we do punish physicians who treat a sick patient "negligently"—and we have turned universities into therapeutic institutions for their students.

Paul Joffe, the psychologist who heads the University of Illinois's suicide-prevention program, explains: "We may have had a program of 'invite and encourage,' but the students had their own program of 'resist and refuse.'" In fact, college suicide prevention programs have nothing to do with preventing suicide: they are charades that give the illusion that the "responsible" parties are behaving responsibly. In the process, they punish the students. "I'd rather get sued for saving a kid's life than for ignoring a kid's life," declares William L. Riley, the university's dean of students. In practice, "saving a kid's life" from suicide typically means that he was stigmatized and locked up as mad.

In fact, evidence indicates that coercive psychiatric suicide prevention increases the incidence of suicide.

As matters stand, the college's liability for the student's suicide is a given. This is a very recent cultural and legal development. Epitomized by the tobacco litigation, American civil law is standing the classic free market principle caveat emptor [(Let the Buyer Beware)] on its head: Caveat vendor [(Let the Seller Beware)].

The law classifies suicide as a "wrongful death." Formerly, the term "wrongful" qualified the conduct of the person who killed himself. Now, it qualifies the conduct of the individuals and institutions that fail to prevent the suicide from killing himself—while he is assumed to have been temporarily insane.

Coercive Suicide Prevention May Increase Suicide Rates

Colleges cannot compel students to attend classes, much less to learn; they can only fail them. . . . Colleges cannot compel students to report to mental health professionals, much less to undergo "counseling"; they can only suspend or expel them. The assumption behind such "therapeutic" coercion is that it is an effective method of preventing suicide. There is not a shred of evidence for this. In fact, evidence indicates that coercive psychiatric suicide prevention increases the incidence of suicide.

Frederick K. Goodwin and Kay Redfield Jamison—enthusiasts for suicide prevention and the authors of the major psychiatric textbook, *Manic-Depressive Illness*—write: "[Some psychiatrists] found that 7 percent of the patients in their sample had committed suicide while in a psychiatric hospital. [Others] reported an even higher rate: 27 percent of manic-depressive patients killed themselves while under hospital care." If incarcerating individuals in insane asylums (and prisons) cannot prevent their killing themselves, how could college personnel prevent the student suicides?

The testimony of individuals subjected to psychiatric incarceration is relevant in this connection. French writer Antonin Artaud (1896–1948) declared: "I myself spent nine years in an insane asylum and I never had the obsession of suicide, but I know that each conversation with a psychiatrist, every morning at the time of his visit, made me want to hang myself, realizing that I would not be able to slit his throat."

We deceive ourselves about the basic, unchanging and unalterable facts of life. Every period—childhood, youth, adulthood, old age—has its travails and tribulations. One of the most difficult periods is youth and young adulthood, when the individual—no longer a child, but not yet a mature adult—is expected to complete the difficult voyage from carefree childhood to responsible adulthood. This voyage may be eased or hindered by others—parents, siblings, teachers—but, in the end, each person must make it on his own. The wonder is that so many do make it, not that some don't. Treating university students as potential mental patients will insure that many more won't make it. Sadly, that may be the intended, not the unintended, consequence of all psychiatric policies preventing mental illness and promoting mental health.

For the subject, suicide is, ipso facto [in itself], a solution for the problems he faces. For the psychiatrist, suicide of the Other—not his own, which is frequent—is a disease to be treated and cured. That disjunction is the source of much perplexity in psychiatry, much profit in law, and much unnecessary suffering for the public.

Suicide is an act, not a disease. Preventing suicide—like preventing drunkenness—is the responsibility of the college student, not the college administration.

Organizations to Contact

The editors have compiled the following list of organizations concerned with the issues debated in this book. The descriptions are derived from materials provided by the organizations. All have publications or information available for interested readers. The list was compiled when the present volume was published; the information provided here may have changed since then. Be aware that many organizations take several weeks or longer to respond to inquiries, so allow as much time as possible.

American Association of Suicidology (AAS)
5221 Wisconsin Avenue NW, Washington, DC   20015
(202) 237-2280 • fax: (202) 237-2282
e-mail: info@suicidology.org
Web site: www.suicidology.org/

The goal of the AAS is to understand and prevent suicide. Founded in 1968, it promotes research, public awareness programs, public education, and training for professionals and volunteers. AAS is also a national clearinghouse for information on suicide. The organization publishes the bimonthly *Suicide and Life-Threatening Behavior*, the quarterly newsletter *Newslink*, the yearly *Annual Conference Proceedings*, and *Directory of Suicide Prevention and Crisis Intervention Agencies in the United States*.

American Foundation for Suicide Prevention (AFSP)
120 Wall Street, 22nd Floor, New York, NY   10005
(888) 333-AFSP • fax: (212) 363-6237
e-mail: inquiry@afsp.org
Web site: www.afsp.org

AFSP is the only national not-for-profit organization exclusively dedicated to understanding and preventing suicide through research and education. It also reaches out to people with mood disorders and those affected by suicide. Since 2000,

AFSP has invested over $6 million in new studies, including research into treatments for people who are depressed and suicidal. The foundation's youth suicide public service announcement "Suicide Shouldn't Be a Secret" airs in 85 television markets nationwide, reaching over 88 million viewers.

American Nurses Association (ANA)
8515 Georgia Avenue, Suite 400, Silver Spring, MD   20910
(800) 274-4262 • fax: (301) 628-5001
e-mail: ethics@ana.org
Web site: www.nursingworld.org/

The American Nurses Association is the only full-service professional organization representing the nation's 2.9 million registered nurses (RNs) through its 54 constituent member associations. The ANA advances the nursing profession by fostering high standards of nursing practice, promoting the economic and general welfare of nurses in the workplace, projecting a positive and realistic view of nursing, and by lobbying the Congress and regulatory agencies on health care issues affecting nurses and the public. The ANA publishes *American Nurses Today, The American Nurse,* and the *American Journal of Nursing.*

American Psychiatric Association
1000 Wilson Boulevard, Suite 1825
Arlington, VA   22209-3901
(800) 368-5777 • fax: (707) 907-7300
e-mail: apa@psych.org
Web site: www.psych.org/

The association is a medical specialty society recognized worldwide. The association's 35,000 U.S. and international member physicians work together to ensure humane care and effective treatment for all persons with mental disorder, including mental retardation and substance-related disorders. It publishes the monthly *American Journal of Psychiatry* and the bimonthly *Psychiatric News.*

American Psychological Association
750 First Street NE, Washington, DC   20002-4242
(800) 374-2721
e-mail: executiveoffice@apa.org
Web site: www.apa.org/

The APA is a scientific and professional organization that represents psychology in the United States. With 150,000 members, the APA is the largest association of psychologists worldwide. Its mission is to advance psychology as a science and
profession and as a means of promoting health, education,
and human welfare. The organization publishes the journal
Psychological Bulletin, numerous children's books and videos,
and other clinical resources.

Compassion & Choices
PO Box 101810, Denver, CO   80250-1810
(800) 247-7421 • fax: (303) 639-1224
e-mail: info@compassionandchoices.org
Web site: www.compassionandchoices.org/

Compassion & Choices seeks to improve care and expand
choice at the end of life. With over 60 chapters nationwide
and 30,000 members, the organization helps patients and their
loved ones face the end of life with facts and choices of action. It is an advocate of legal reform to promote pain care,
strengthen advance directives, and legalize physician assisted
suicide. Every quarter it publishes *Compassion & Choices
Magazine*.

Euthanasia Prevention Coalition
Box 25033, London, Ontario
N6C6A8
Canada
(877) 439-3348 • fax: (519) 439-7053
e-mail: info@epcc.ca
Web site: www.epcc.ca/

The Euthanasia Prevention Coalition opposes any attempt to
legalize euthanasia or assisted suicide or any legislation that
will lead to the further devaluing of human life. It seeks to

prepare a well-informed, broadly-based network of organizations and individuals that will create an effective social barrier to euthanasia and assisted suicide. It also strives to enhance government support for hospice/palliative care. The organization publishes a monthly newsletter and offers several public use pamphlets.

Final Exit Network
PO Box 965005, Marietta, GA   30066
(800) 524-3948
e-mail: info@finalexitnetwork.org
Web site: www.finalexitnetwork.org/

Final Exit Network is a volunteer organization dedicated to serving people who are suffering from an intolerable medical condition and want to kill themselves. Volunteers provide counseling, support, and guidance to self-deliverance at a time and place of a person's choosing. However, the organization does not encourage individuals to hasten their death. It offers interested people *Exit Guides* and has First Responders located across the country.

Human Rights Campaign
1640 Rhode Island Avenue NW
Washington, DC   20036-3278
(800) 777-4723 • fax: (202) 347-5323
e-mail: hrc@hrc.org
Web site: www.hrc.org

The Human Rights Campaign (HRC) is America's largest civil rights organization working to achieve gay, lesbian, bisexual and transgender (GLBT) equality. HRC lobbies Congress, provides campaign support to like-minded candidates, and works to educate the public on a wide array of topics affecting GLBT Americans, including relationship recognition, workplace, family, and health issues. The Campaign publishes the *Equality Update Newsletter*, and *Generation EQ*, a newsletter for young GLBT and allied people.

National Association of Lesbian, Gay, Bisexual, and Transgender Community Centers (NALGBTCC)

1325 Massachusetts Avenue NW, Suite 600
Washington, DC 20005
(202) 824-0450 • fax: (202) 393-2241
e-mail: terry@lgbtcenters.org
Web site: www.lgbtcenters.org

The National Association of LGBT Community Centers envisions a society that celebrates diversity, acknowledges the dignity of LGBT people, and embraces full human rights for all citizens. The association creates networking opportunities for community center leaders, offering peer-based technical assistance and training to centers, helps communities to launch and grow new centers, and offers program solutions and materials that meet the needs of member centers throughout the country.

National Hospice and Palliative Care Organization

1700 Diagonal Road, Suite 625, Alexandria, VA 22314
(703) 837-1500 • fax: (703) 837-1233
e-mail: nhpco_info@nhpco.org
Web site: www.nhpco.org

The National Hospice and Palliative Care Organization is the largest nonprofit membership organization representing hospice and palliative care programs and professionals in the country. Opposed to euthanasia and assisted suicide, the association's mission is to improve end of life care and expand access to hospice care for people dying and their loved ones in the United States. The association offers its members online newsletters.

National Right to Life Committee

512 10th St. NW, Washington, DC 20004
(202) 626-8800
e-mail: nrlc@nrlc.org
Web site: www.nrlc.org

NRLC believes that euthanasia is the intentional killing by act or omission of a dependent human being for his or her alleged benefit. The committee's ultimate goal is to restore legal protection to innocent human life. It is also concerned with related matters of medical ethics, which relate to the right to life issues of euthanasia and infanticide. It publishes *NRL News*. It also e-mails up-to-the-minute alerts that deal with breaking pro-life news.

Samaritans
The Upper Mill, Kingston Road, Ewell, Surrey KT17
England
+44 (0)20 8394 8300 • fax: +44 (0)20 8394 8301
e-mail: admin@samaritans.org
Web site: www.samaritans.org

The Samaritans is the largest suicide prevention organization in the world. It provides confidential emotional support to any person who is suicidal or in despair. It also seeks to increase public awareness of issues around suicide and depression. It has branches in over 50 countries and the Web site is available in 15 languages. It offers numerous online publications relating to self-harm, stress, depression, suicide, and mental health problems.

United States Conference of Catholic Bishops (USCCB)
3211 4th Street NE, Washington, DC 20017-1194
(202) 541-3000
e-mail: prolife@usccb.org
Web site: www.usccb.org

The United States Conference of Catholic Bishops believe that human life is a precious gift from God; that each person who receives this gift has responsibilities toward God, self and others; and that society, through its laws and social institutions, must protect and nurture human life at every stage of its existence. The Catholic Church publishes numerous pro-life documents, including *Life Insight, Life at Risk*, and *Natural Family Planning*.

University of Pennsylvania Center for Bioethics
3401 Market Street, Suite 320, Philadelphia, PA   19104-3308
(215) 898-7136 • fax: (215) 573-3036
Web site: www.bioethics.upenn.edu/

The field of bioethics provides a practical language for mediating between developments in science and popular culture and a means for our society to talk about its deepest moral concerns, fears, and hopes. With this in mind, the Center for Bioethics promotes scholarly and public understanding of the ethical, legal, social, and public policy implications of advances in the life sciences and medicine. The center publishes a biannual newsletter called *PennBioethics*, which combines short informative articles, opinion pieces, and updates on the activities of the center faculty.

Bibliography

Books

Margaret Pabst Battin	*Ending Life: Ethics and the Way We Die.* New York: Oxford University Press, 2005.
David Chidester	*Salvation and Suicide: Jim Jones, the Peoples Temple, and Jonestown.* Bloomington: Indiana University Press, 2003.
Loren Coleman	*The Copycat Effect: How the Media and Popular Culture Trigger the Mayhem in Tomorrow's Headlines.* New York: Paraview Pocket Books, 2004.
George Howe Colt	*November of the Soul: The Enigma of Suicide.* New York: Scribner, 2006.
Bernard Cooper	*The Bill from My Father: A Memoir.* New York: Simon & Schuster, 2006.
David Cox and Candy Arrington	*Aftershock: Help, Hope, and Healing in the Wake of Suicide,* Nashville, TN: Broadman & Holman, 2003.
Michel Dorais, Simon L. Lajeunesse, and Pierre Tremblay	*Dead Boys Can't Dance: Sexual Orientation, Masculinity, and Suicide.* Montreal: McGill-Queen's University Press, 2004.
Kathleen M. Foley and Herbert Hendin	*The Case against Assisted Suicide: For the Right to End-of-Life Care.* Baltimore: The Johns Hopkins University Press, 2004.

Curtis Gay

The Funny Thing About Suicide. Bloomington, IN: Authorhouse, 2006.

Neil M. Gorsuch

The Future of Assisted Suicide and Euthanasia. Princeton, NJ: Princeton University Press, 2006.

Dell P. Hackett and John M. Violanti (eds.)

Police Suicide: Tactics for Prevention. Springfield, IL: Charles C. Thomas, 2003.

Helen Hays

Surviving Suicide: Help to Heal Your Heart—Life Stories from Those Left Behind. Dallas, TX: Brown Books, 2005.

Albert Y. Hsu

Grieving a Suicide: A Loved One's Search for Comfort, Answers and Hope. Downer's Grove, IL: InterVarsity Press, 2002.

Tom Hunt

Cliffs of Despair: A Journey to the Edge. New York: Random House, 2006.

Thomas Joiner

Why People Die by Suicide. Cambridge, MA: Harvard University Press, 2006.

Farhad Khosrokhavar and David Macey

Suicide Bombers: Allah's New Martyrs. London: Pluto Press, 2005.

Jon Kilmo and Pamela Rae Heath

Suicide: What Really Happens in the Afterlife? Berkeley, CA: North Atlantic Books, 2006.

June Cerza Kolf *Standing in the Shadow: Help and Encouragement for Suicide Survivors.* Grand Rapids, MI: Baker Books, 2002.

David Lester *Fixin' to Die: A Compassionate Guide to Committing Suicide or Staying Alive.* Amityville, NY: Baywood Publishing, 2003.

Duncan Osborne *Suicide Tuesday: Gay Men and the Crystal Meth Scare.* New York: Carroll & Graf, 2005.

Robert Pape *Dying to Win: The Strategic Logic of Suicide Terrorism.* New York: Random House, 2006.

Margo Requarth *After a Parent's Suicide: Helping Children Heal.* Sabastopol, CA: Healing Hearts Press, 2006.

Christoph Reuter *My Life Is a Weapon: A Modern History of Suicide Bombing.* Princeton, NJ: Princeton University Press, 2006.

E. Betsy Ross and Joseph Richman *After Suicide: A Ray of Hope for Those Left Behind.* Reading, MA: Perseus Publishing, 2002.

Donna Simmons *A Fork in the Road: My Story of Suicide and Survival.* Victoria, BC: Trafford, 2006.

Rosemarie Skaine *Female Suicide Bombers.* Jefferson, NC: McFarland, 2006.

Wesley Smith   *Culture of Death: The Assault on Medical Ethics in America.* San Francisco: Encounter Books, 2002.

Mark Steyn   *America Alone: The End of the World As We Know It.* Washington, DC: Regnery Publishing, 2006.

Thomas Szasz   *Fatal Freedom: The Ethics and Politics of Suicide.* Syracuse, NY: Syracuse University Press, 2002.

Barbara Victor   *Army of Roses: Inside the World of Palestinian Women Suicide Bombers.* Emmaus, PA: Rodale Books, 2003.

Periodicals

Alao, Adekola O. et al.   "Cybersuicide: Review of the Role of the Internet on Suicide," *CyberPsychology and Behavior,* 2006.

Donna Barnes   "The Aftermath of Suicide Among African Americans," *Journal of Black Psychology,* 2006.

David Bukay   "The Religious Foundations of Suicide Bombings," *Middle East Quarterly,* Fall 2006.

Ronald P. Byars   "Deuteronomy 6:1–15 (Between Text & Sermon)," *Interpretation,* April 2006.

Laura Coleman   "Kentucky Program Cuts Suicide Rate in Jails," *State News,* November–December 2006.

Anthony R.
D'Augelli et al.

"Predicting the Suicide Attempts of Lesbian, Gay, and Bisexual Youth," *Suicide and Life-Threatening Behavior*, 2005.

Denise D. Denton

"In Apparent Suicide, Chancellor Dies in a Fall," *Chronicle of Higher Education*, July 7, 2006.

Paul Duberstein
and Marnin J.
Heisel

"Suicide in Older Adults: How Do We Detect Risk and What Can We Do About It?," *Psychiatric Times*, November 2006.

Bruce Gross

"Global Suicide," *Forensic Examiner*, Summer 2006.

Roisin Healy

"Suicide in Early Modern and Modern Europe," *Historical Journal*, 2006.

Melody K.
Hoffman

"What Really Happened: T.O.'s 'Attempted Suicide' That Wasn't," *Jet*, October 16, 2006.

E. Jaffe

"Deadly Disorder: Imagined-Ugliness Illness Yields High Suicide Rate," *Science News*, July 2006.

David Lester

"Can Suicide Be a Good Death?" *Death Studies*, 2006.

Henry
Morgenstern

"Suicide Terror: Is Law Enforcement Ready?" *Law Enforcement Technology*, September 2006.

Mutsuhiro Nakao and Takeaki Takeuchia — "The Suicide Epidemic in Japan and Strategies of Depression Screening for Its Prevention," *Bulletin of the World Health Organization*, June 2006.

William Pridemore — "Heavy Drinking and Suicide in Russia," *Social Forces*, September 2006.

Chitra Ragavan — "Suicide Bomb Scare," *U.S. News & World Report*, July 2006.

Katie Sandbrook — "Suicide: Cry for Help or Selfish Act," *Indian Life*, September–October 2006.

Allan J. Schwartz — "College Student Suicide in the United States: 1990–1991 through 2003–2004," *Journal of American College Health*, May–June 2006.

Andrew Silke — "The Role of Suicide in Politics, Conflict, and Terrorism," *Terrorism and Political Violence*, 2006.

Marisa Spann et al. — "Suicide and African American Teenagers: Risk Factors and Coping Mechanisms," *Suicide and Life-Threatening Behavior*, 2006.

Kevin Spurgaitis — "Dying Young: The Skyrocketing Rate of First Nations Youth Suicide Shows No Signs of Falling," *Catholic New Times*, July 2006.

United Press International — "Suicide Bomber Identified as Grandmother," *UPI NewsTrack*, November 24, 2006.

John S. Westefeld and others — "College Student Suicide: A Call to Action," *Death Studies*, 2006.

——— "High School Suicide: Knowledge and Opinions of Teachers," *Journal of Loss & Trama*, 2007.

Shaun Whittaker — "Suicide and Unemployment," *Africa News Service*, November 3, 2006.

Masood Zangeneh and Teri Hason — "Suicide and Gambling," *International Journal of Mental Health and Addiction*, 2006.

Internet Resources

Patrick J. Buchanan — "The Assisted Suicide of the West," *Townhall.com*, April 22, 2002 at: http://www.townhall.com/columnists/PatrickJBuchanan/2002/04/22/the_assisted_suicide_of_the_west

Audrey Kurth Cronin — "Terrorists and Suicide Attacks," *Congressional Research Service*, August 28, 2003 at: www.fas.org/irp/crs/RL32058.pdf

Sherman B. Nuland — "The Principal of Hope," *New Republic Online*, May 22, 2002 at: www.tnr.com/doc.mhtml?i=20020527&s=nuland052702

Herman Schwartz — "Legal Legacy," *The Nation*, October 12, 2006 at: www.thenation.com/doc/20061030/schwartz

Peter Singer

"Freedom and the Right to Die," *Free Inquiry*, May 15, 2002 at: www.utilitarian.net/singer/by/ 20020515.htm

Wesley J. Smith

"Respectable Baby Killing: Support Builds for Legalizing Euthanasia for Ill and Newborn Babies," *National Review Online,* November 16, 2006 at: http://article.nationalreview.com/ ?q=NzQ4ODllNzE2YTcxNTIzNzgz NDc5NGQlYTk1Njk4NTA=

Index